The **Women's Health** Book

D1439423

Disclaimer

This book is designed to increase knowledge, awareness and understanding of women's health issues. It is not intended to replace the advice that your own doctor can give you. If you are concerned by any of the issues raised in this book make sure you consult your GP, who is there to help you.

Whilst every effort has been made to ensure the accuracy of the information and material contained in this book, nevertheless it is possible that errors or omissions may occur in the content. The author and publishers assume no responsibility for and give no guarantees or warranties concerning the accuracy, completeness or up-to-date nature of the information provided in this book.

The **Women's Health** Book

A Guide for the Irish Woman

Dr Rachel Mackey

ORPEN PRESS

Published by
Orpen Press
Lonsdale House
Avoca Avenue
Blackrock
Co. Dublin
Ireland

e-mail: info@orpenpress.com
www.orpenpress.com

Paperback ISBN: 978-1-871305-87-6
ePub ISBN: 978-1-909518-11-7
Kindle ISBN: 978-1-909518-12-4

Printed and bound by CPI Group (UK) Ltd, Croydon, CR0 4YY

Acknowledgements

I would like to thank Elizabeth Brennan, Eileen O'Brien and Jennifer Thompson at Orpen Press for all their assistance with this book; thanks also to Jean Harrington. I am very grateful to Dr Peter McKenna for writing the foreword. I would especially like to thank Declan for all his incredible patience and kindness while I wrote; I could not have finished it without his help. Finally, I would like to thank my children, Alice, Charlotte, Sam and Joe, for their love and support.

Dr Rachel Mackey – About the Author

Rachel Mackey is a women's health specialist. She graduated from the Royal College of Surgeons in Ireland in 1992, winning the JB Lyons Medal in Medicine. She specialised in obstetrics and gynaecology and became a member of the Royal College of Obstetricians and Gynaecologists in 2000. As part of her training she completed three years of research at the Royal Hospital for Women in Sydney, Australia in the area of the menopause and reproductive endocrinology. In April 2007, drawing on her extensive obstetric and gynaecological expertise, she opened the Women's Health Clinic in Dun Laoghaire, County Dublin, which offers a wide range of health services to women.

Dr Mackey has published a number of articles both in medical journals and in the medical press on a wide range of topics in the area of women's health, including original research.

She is the mother of four children and enjoys running and playing hockey.

Contents

Foreword

We live in an era of rapid access to information, data and opinion, all of which is readily available through the internet. This information, whilst rich in detail, may lack both balance and perspective, and it is my sense that this tendency towards a lack of perspective may be exacerbated by not knowing the right questions to ask. *The Women's Health Book* provides a wealth of information that will support women to 'ask the right questions' and comes with the added benefit of Dr Mackey's vast clinical experience in dealing with clients presenting with the issues described herein.

This is not a textbook of obstetrics and gynaecology – it is a useful compendium of symptomatology, presenting complaints and enquiries for which many women seek advice. In many ways it must have been more difficult to decide what to leave out of such a book rather than what to include. There are many variations of disease progression that are related to gender, even in diseases that do not appear to be gender specific. That said, those topics which are considered to have a particular female interest are covered systematically, clearly and concisely in this book. Dr Mackey tackles her subject in a no-nonsense, easy-to-read style, and her empathy with the concerns of women in the context of their health is apparent throughout.

Dr Peter McKenna
Consultant Obstetrician and Gynaecologist
Rotunda Hospital, Dublin

Preface

When I was approached to write this book it struck me that there was so little information available to women specifically about women's health. Women are fantastic patients to work with because they are so interested in their own health and keen to educate themselves about their bodies and what can go wrong. So many times in my own clinic, however, women have told me that they had struggled to find information on their particular problem until they came to see me. The advent of the internet has, in many ways, been incredibly helpful to women in the area of their health, but often the information can be inaccurate and confusing.

I wanted to write a book that would be clear and informative for all generations of women – the kind of book you can dip in and out of, depending on your stage in life and your particular symptoms at any one time. In this book I have covered many different problems that I see in everyday practice in my clinic. Nevertheless, I could not cover everything, so I apologise in advance to those of you who cannot find your specific problem in this book. In particular, pregnancy is such a huge topic that I could not discuss it in any great detail, but I have provided an overview of it.

I very much enjoyed putting my experience and knowledge of women's health down on paper, and I hope you find this book useful both for yourself and your family, now and in years to come.

All royalties from this book will go to Breast Cancer Ireland. Breast Cancer Ireland is a charity established to raise vital funding to support research into breast cancer. The goal at Breast Cancer Ireland is to seek to transform breast cancer from often being a fatal disease to a chronic illness that can be managed long term through treatment.

1

Weight Issues

This is probably the most important chapter in this book in terms of women's health. The effects on your body of being overweight can be seen in almost every chapter, so this is the key to wellbeing in every aspect of living: physically, psychologically, sexually and emotionally.

Obesity

Being overweight or obese is defined by body mass index (BMI). This is calculated by dividing your weight in kilograms by your height in metres squared (kg/m^2).

Scary Facts about Irish Women's Weight

- 33 per cent of Irish women are overweight; the highest proportion of these is in the 51 to 64-year-old age group.
- 26 per cent of Irish women are obese.
- 22 per cent of our children are overweight or obese.

Obesity occurs when there is an imbalance between the amount of calories consumed and the amount of calories burned through exercise. The problem has become an epidemic in developed countries over the last few decades because of our poor lifestyle choices, and is threatening our health in a variety of different ways. Being overweight can lead to an increased risk of the following:

- Heart disease
- Stroke
- Diabetes
- High blood pressure
- Breathing problems
- Arthritis
- Gallbladder disease
- Some cancers, such as breast and uterine
- Infertility and obesity-related problems in pregnancy

But excess body weight isn't the only health risk. How you store your body fat also affects your health. Women with a 'pear' shape tend to store fat on their hips and bottoms. Women with an 'apple' shape store fat around their waists. This is called visceral fat and increases your risk of heart disease to a greater extent than fat stored on hips and bottoms. If your waist is more than 35 inches, you may have a higher risk of weight-related health problems.

The following are the various treatment options available for obesity, but not all of these are necessarily needed:

- Dietary changes
- Exercise and activity
- Behaviour changes; in other words, change your habits
- Prescription weight-loss medications
- Weight-loss surgery

Weight Issues

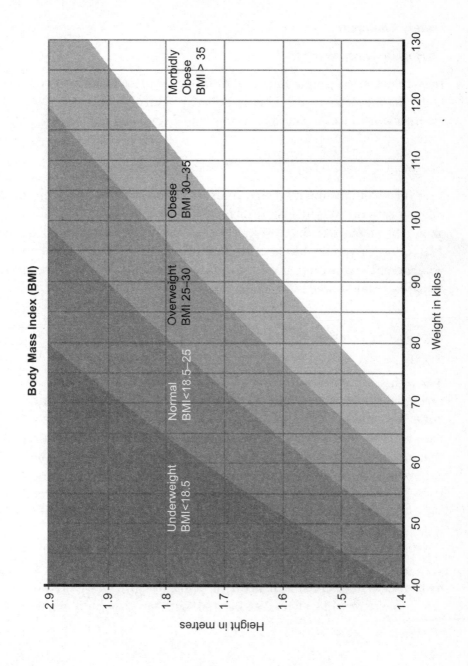

Dietary Changes

So How Do I Lose Weight?

It is a very simple equation: you *must* put fewer calories into your body than you burn off. This is done by limiting the amount of calories you consume and increasing your exercising activities.

How Many Calories a Day Should I Consume to Lose Weight?

It is very well documented that in order to lose weight and keep it off, the rate of weight loss needs to be slow and controlled. This should be no more than 0.5–1 kg (1–2 lbs) per week. In order to lose 1 lb per week you should be eating 500 fewer calories per day than you currently consume; in order to lose 2 lbs per week you should be eating 1,000 fewer calories per day.

Why Shouldn't I Follow the Diet that Promises 10 lbs Weight Loss in Ten Days?

These diets either require a very low calorie intake per day, or a low carbohydrate intake. While you may see dramatic results instantly with these diets, a very low calorie diet causes the body's metabolism to slow down temporarily; the body is fooled into thinking that it is being starved and slows down fat burning to protect itself from starvation. This results in tiredness and a lack of energy. It also means that when you do return to any kind of normal calorie intake, you will gain weight quickly until your metabolism bounces back.

With low carbohydrate diets the protein content of the diet is very high, and the body is forced into burning fat instead of carbohydrates for fuel. This will result in some weight loss, but there are unpleasant side effects associated with a very high protein diet, such as bad breath, constipation and cramps. The eventual re-introduction of carbohydrates to the diet results in inevitable weight gain.

With both of these diets the sudden dramatic weight loss can be attributed to loss of water from the body, which is temporary. This is because the body needs to use a lot of its water to wash out the by-products of fat burning, leading to a diuretic effect. This gives an impression of sudden dramatic weight loss, which is not sustained over time.

Experts all agree that it is a reduction in calories overall with a good balance between carbohydrates, fats and protein which will yield the best results in the long term.

What Should I Eat?

The truth is that as long as it is not a quick-fix weight-loss diet it doesn't matter which 'diet' you follow, the important thing is to stick to it. The most successful way to lose weight is to see it as a permanent change in the way you live your life; this includes the way you shop and cook, and the introduction of exercise into your daily routine. Once you view your diet like that, then you will succeed, because you have a long-term plan.

You will find that the list of foods you should be eating is pretty much the same with all healthy eating plans. But remember, you must control your portions: you may be eating healthy food, but if you eat too much of it, the weight won't come off. Healthy foods include the following:

- Wholegrains, such as wholewheat pasta, brown rice, high-fibre cereals, multigrain or wholewheat breads, and porridge
- Protein, such as lean chicken, fish, limited red meat intake, beans and nuts

- Fruit and vegetables – all of them! They are so high in fibre and water that you will feel full long before you have overdone it with the calories.
- Fats – the 'good types' include olive oil, sunflower oil, avocado, nuts, oily fish like tuna, mackerel and sardines.
- Fibre, which is a component of wholegrains, fruit and vegetables, and beans. Fibre is bulky and fills you up quicker; it also keeps you feeling fuller for longer. By eating a lot of fibre you will not feel hungry and deprived of food, making it easier for you to stick to your healthy eating plan.

Exercise and Activity

Exercise alone without a calorie-controlled eating plan is unlikely to succeed. However, it is an essential part of a weight-loss plan, as well as being excellent for your general health.

Get Moving

- You should perform 20 to 30 minutes of moderate exercise, five to seven days a week, preferably daily. Types of exercise include walking, stationary cycling, stair climbing machines, jogging and swimming.
- Exercise can be broken up into shorter, 10-minute sessions.
- Start slowly and progress gradually to avoid injury, excessive soreness or fatigue. Over time, build up to between 30 and 60 minutes of moderate to vigorous exercise every day.

Behaviour Changes

Research has shown that you are more likely to succeed in changing your eating habits for the better if you get support. This can mean getting a friend to start your new regime with you or joining a weight-loss group, such as Weight Watchers or Unislim. Women are more likely to succeed when they are supported by other people.

Change the Way You Eat

- Try not to have treats lying around – out of sight, out of mind!
- Plan your meals ahead.
- Cook your own meals at home.
- Stop eating before you are full; it takes a few minutes for your brain to register that your stomach is full.
- Think about the times that you overeat: is it when you are stressed, upset or lonely? Find another way to comfort yourself emotionally, for example through yoga, meditation, a new activity or exercise.

Weight-loss Medication

Your doctor may recommend using weight-loss medication if you are not losing weight through diet and exercise alone, or if your BMI is above 27 and you have weight-related issues, such as sleep apnoea, diabetes or high blood pressure. Orlistat (Alli) is available without prescription and works by preventing the absorption of fat through the gut. After one year of medication, the average weight loss is only 2–3 kg more than you would get from diet and exercise alone.

Surgery

Weight-loss surgery is also known as bariatric surgery. These procedures can be extremely effective in achieving significant weight loss, but they can also be high risk, due to complications associated with operating on overweight patients. They work by reducing the amount of food that can be comfortably eaten, by reducing the absorption rate of food, or both.

They are most suitable for:

- Women with a BMI greater than 40
- Women with a BMI of between 35 and 39 who have significant health problems, such as diabetes or high blood pressure

The two most common bariatric surgeries offered are:

- Gastric bypass surgery – a loop of small intestine is connected to a new pouch created at the top of the stomach, allowing most of the ingested food and liquid to bypass the stomach.
- Gastric banding – this is less invasive and is done through keyhole surgery. It creates a band around the stomach, which divides the stomach into two small pouches. The tightness of the band can be adjusted, depending on the size of stomach required for weight loss. This procedure will not work without behavioural changes and, therefore, has a lower success rate than other procedures.

Bariatric surgery is an extreme answer to an extreme problem. The patient is required to have tried every other form of weight loss before resorting to major surgery. Like all weight-loss plans, the patient must be totally committed to a new way of healthy living. It should be viewed only as a last resort. Life changes dramatically after these surgeries: food as you know it is no longer possible. Meals must be liquid-only initially and will always have to be very small. Vitamin supplements are sometimes necessary with bypass surgery, as vitamin absorption can often be affected.

Weight Gain After the Menopause

Most women will notice that as they get older they find it progressively harder to lose weight. This becomes much more noticeable around the menopause. A lot of women feel that it is beyond their control and 'the hormones' are responsible; however, it is not inevitable. The hormonal changes associated with the menopause are mostly responsible for the development of fat around the abdomen, even where it was never there before.

What Causes It?

There are several reasons why weight gain can occur around the time of the menopause, and they are almost all preventable. These include:

- Loss of muscle mass – as you get older the amount of muscle in your body naturally reduces. Muscle is very efficient at burning calories and, therefore, as you lose muscle your body composition will shift to more fat than muscle. This means that if you do not work on maintaining your muscle mass you will gradually put on weight, even though you are not eating any more than before.
- Emotional factors, such as children leaving home, divorce or the death of a spouse or loved one, can cause you to overeat for comfort.
- Contentment or simply 'letting yourself go' can lead to weight gain.
- Genetic factors may play a role in some women.

Achieve Weight Loss Around the Menopause

You lose weight around the menopause the same way you do at any age. Therefore, to lose weight you should:

- Exercise more – you need to do at least 30 minutes of exercise daily, plus a couple of sessions of strength training per week to maintain muscle mass. You may even need to do more than this to achieve specific weight-loss goals.
- Eat less – you need 200 calories fewer per day in your fifties than in your thirties or forties. You should be eating lean protein, fruit, vegetables and wholegrains. Avoid skipping meals, as this may lead to overeating later.
- Seek support – women do better with family and friends supporting them to change their lifestyle.

Diabetes

Our bodies are very efficient at converting the food that we eat to energy to fuel our activities. Sugars or carbohydrates are transported from the bloodstream into the cells of the body, where the sugar is burned to make energy. Insulin is the hormone which controls this system, and is produced by the pancreas.

Diabetes is a condition where insulin is either no longer being produced or the body becomes resistant to insulin. This leads to high blood sugar levels or hyperglycaemia.

What Are Type 1 and Type 2 Diabetes?

Type 1 diabetes is the diabetes typically associated with children. There are approximately 14,000 type 1 diabetics in Ireland. It is usually diagnosed in childhood and is due to a complete absence of insulin. It is possible that it is an autoimmune disease; in other words the body produces antibodies to itself, causing insulin production to fail at a young age. People with type 1 diabetes require insulin replacement for life, either through self-injecting or an insulin pump.

Type 2 diabetes is more relevant to this chapter, as there is a direct link between obesity and the development of type 2 diabetes. The prevalence of this kind of diabetes has been increasing dramatically over recent years, due to the obesity epidemic that is gripping the first world. In Ireland, it is estimated that there are between 140,000 and 160,000 people with known type 2 diabetes, and a further 30,000 with undiagnosed type 2 diabetes.

Risk Factors for Type 2 Diabetes

Certain factors increase your risk of developing type 2 diabetes. These include:

- Obesity
- Sedentary lifestyle

- Diabetes in pregnancy or delivering a baby weighing more than 4 kg (9 lbs)
- Poor diet
- Being over the age of 45

Signs and Symptoms of Type 2 Diabetes

Symptoms to watch out for include:

- Excessive thirstiness
- Waking at night to urinate
- Headaches
- Recurrent urinary tract infections (UTIs)
- Recurrent skin infections

In a lot of cases, however, the symptoms are very minimal and the patient may not feel unwell enough to mention it to their doctor. The average length of time between the onset of type 2 diabetes and diagnosis is twelve years. Unfortunately, a lot of irreversible damage can be done to the body from high blood sugar during that time. If you feel that you are at risk of diabetes, it is essential to have your blood sugar level checked, preferably after fasting for 12 hours. This test will immediately show whether you have diabetes. It may also show a pre-diabetic picture, which means that with life-style alterations it is possible for you to stop the development of full-blown diabetes by losing weight, exercising and changing your eating habits permanently.

Complications of Diabetes

Sustained high blood sugar levels cause damage to many organs over time, leading to blindness, kidney damage and failure, nerve damage and ensuing numbness in the feet. It damages blood vessels, which can cause heart disease and peripheral vascular disease, which may eventually lead to amputations.

Management of Type 2 Diabetes

Type 2 diabetes is managed with a combination of diet, exercise and medication. About 40 per cent of type 2 diabetics will end up using insulin. Overall wellbeing for diabetics also includes regular eye examinations and careful foot care.

What Can I Do to Prevent This?

The answer to this is simple – change your lifestyle now. Up to 50 per cent of cases of type 2 diabetes are preventable by losing weight and exercising.

Key Points

- Obesity is increasing in Irish women at an alarming rate.
- Being obese greatly increases your risk of heart disease, stroke, diabetes and cancer.
- Your BMI should be between 19 and 25.
- In order to successfully lose weight you need to restrict your calorie intake, exercise regularly and change your behaviour around food.
- Medication and surgery can be used as a last resort.
- Type 2 diabetes in women is increasing as a direct result of obesity.

2

Thyroid Problems

The Thyroid Gland

The thyroid gland is a hormone-producing gland found in the neck, overlying the windpipe. It is an essential gland, producing thyroid hormones which have an effect on every cell in our bodies. The gland produces two hormones – T3 and T4 – using iodine which has been absorbed from food, such as seafood, salt and bread. Thyroid hormones are needed for energy and also to control growth and the production of other hormones in the body.

Problems arising in the thyroid gland occur far more often in women than in men. The more common thyroid disorders are described in this chapter.

Underactive Thyroid (Hypothyroidism)

An underactive thyroid gland is six times more common in women than in men, and figures suggest that between 1 and 4 per cent of women will develop it at some stage in their lives. The problem becomes much more common as women get older. The symptoms of hypothyroidism are easy to miss, as they can easily be mistaken for something else, especially in the earlier stages of the condition.

The Thyroid Gland

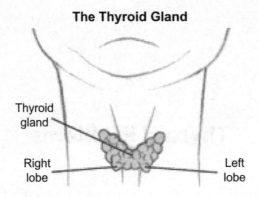

Thyroid gland

Right lobe

Left lobe

Symptoms of Hypothyroidism

The signs and symptoms of hypothyroidism include:

- Tiredness
- Small weight gain
- Intolerance to cold
- Constipation
- Coarse hair
- Dry skin
- Depression
- Excessive sleepiness
- Raised cholesterol readings in blood tests

If hypothyroidism is left untreated and allowed to reach a critical point, heart failure and coma can occur.

Causes of Hypothyroidism

Hashimoto's Disease

This is the most common cause of an underactive thyroid gland and, again, is much more common in women than in men. It is an autoimmune disease, i.e. your body produces antibodies and attacks your own body. In the case of Hashimoto's disease, large amounts of antibody (anti-TPO) are produced against an enzyme called thyroid peroxidase, which is necessary for the production of thyroid hormone. It is diagnosed by testing levels of the antibody in the blood.

Post-partum Thyroiditis

This is a mild form of inflammation seen in the thyroid gland following pregnancy, and it can affect up to 8 per cent of all pregnant women. It often results in a short phase of overproduction of the thyroid hormone, followed by underproduction for up to six months. Normal thyroid function usually returns in time.

Following Treatment of Overactive Thyroid (Hyperthyroidism)

The two treatment options used to treat hyperthyroidism cause either destruction or removal of large amounts of the thyroid tissue. In some cases radioactive iodine is used, and in other cases the affected parts of the gland are removed during surgery. If the thyroid gland has not resumed working within six months of treatment, lifelong thyroid hormone replacement is usually needed.

Pituitary or Hypothalamic Disease

The thyroid gland is controlled by a complex hormone-signalling system involving two areas of the brain: the pituitary gland, which is found behind the nose, and the hypothalamus, which is found deep inside the brain. The production of thyroid hormones depends on both these areas, and if either is damaged, such as during brain surgery or due to a large blood loss, then thyroid function is affected.

Medication

Medications used to treat hyperthyroidism (such as carbimazole) and psychiatric drugs such as lithium, as well as amiodarone, which is used in cardiac conditions, can cause a reduction in thyroid hormone production.

How Is Hypothyroidism Diagnosed?

Hypothyroidism is diagnosed mostly by an analysis of the patient's medical history and by a physical examination of the patient. A blood test will confirm the diagnosis. A hormone called thyroid-stimulating hormone (TSH), which is produced in the pituitary gland, will be abnormally high. When the thyroid gland is not functioning properly, the pituitary gland starts to produce large amounts of TSH in an effort to stimulate the thyroid into action. The level of TSH starts to rise before the level of thyroid hormones – T3 and T4 – starts to drop. Thyroid antibody levels should be checked, and scans of the thyroid gland should be taken if needed.

In most cases of hypothyroidism the reality is that you will need lifelong replacement of the thyroid hormone T4, which is given in a once-daily tablet form. T4 is converted to T3 in the body, so taking it means that both hormones are effectively replaced. Initially when starting thyroid replacement therapy, levels of TSH should be checked every six weeks until the correct dose has been found. Your TSH level should be kept in the region of 1 mmol/L to maintain normal thyroid activity. Once your blood level is stable, it can be checked every six to twelve months.

Overactive Thyroid (Hyperthyroidism)

Hyperthyroidism occurs when the thyroid gland overproduces thyroid hormone. The term thyrotoxicosis is also used, but this includes all causes of increased thyroid hormone in the body, including taking excessive thyroid hormone medication.

Symptoms of Hyperthyroidism

Common symptoms seen with hyperthyroidism include:

- Excessive sweating and intolerance to heat
- Weight loss
- Diarrhoea
- Tiredness
- Irregular, light periods
- Tremor
- Muscle weakness
- Increased redness in palms
- Palpitations
- Warm, moist skin
- Itchy, painless rash
- Swelling of the neck

Causes of Hyperthyroidism

The main causes of hyperthyroidism are:

- Graves' disease
- Thyroid nodules
- Thyroiditis
- Excessive intake of thyroid hormone
- Excessive intake of iodine

Graves' Disease

This is the most common cause of hyperthyroidism. It is an autoimmune disease which causes loss of control of hormone production by the thyroid gland, leading to an overproduction of hormones. It is much more common in women than in men. It can be associated with eye symptoms, where eyes can become irritated and bulging. A painless skin rash can also be seen with Graves' disease.

Thyroid Nodules

Occasionally, lumps can form within the thyroid gland itself. They can start to produce thyroid hormone in excessive amounts, leading to hyperthyroidism. If several hormone-producing lumps form, this is known as toxic multinodular goitre.

Thyroiditis

This was mentioned above under hypothyroidism, where the gland can become inflamed and temporarily become overactive, followed by a period of hypothyroidism. The most common types of thyroiditis are associated with a viral illness or following pregnancy. The period of overactivity can last between four and twelve weeks, and the subsequent hypothyroidism can last for a further six months. Most women will regain normal thyroid function.

Excessive Intake of Thyroid Hormone

This can occur where patients on long-term thyroid hormone replacement therapy are not being closely monitored, and their thyroid hormone replacement is excessive.

Excessive Intake of Iodine

An excess of iodine can cause hyperthyroidism, but this usually only occurs in patients who have an underlying thyroid disease. Also, some medications, such as amiodarone which is used in cardiac conditions, contain a lot of iodine and can cause thyroid production problems.

Diagnosis of Hyperthyroidism

Hyperthyroidism is diagnosed initially with blood tests. The TSH reading will be very low, usually reported as undetectable. T3 and T4 levels will be raised. The cause of the hyperthyroidism can then be identified by checking antibody levels, in the case of Graves' disease, and a thyroid scan using radioactive iodine to identify any overactive nodules or lumps within the gland.

Treatment of Hyperthyroidism

Medication

This is usually in the form of carbimazole. This is a drug which blocks thyroid production. It is initially monitored closely, on a monthly basis, to adjust the dose as required to re-establish normal thyroid hormone levels. A rare complication of this drug in less than 1 per cent of patients results in agranulocytosis, a reduced production of white blood cells, which help fight infection. You are warned to contact your doctor if you develop a sore throat or fever while taking carbimazole, and a simple test can check your white blood cell levels. Carbimazole is for long-term use only with Graves' disease, as more than 50 per cent of patients with Graves' disease will go into remission within one to two years. Some doctors will use thyroid replacement therapy at the same time as using carbimazole, which has been shown to have good success. After treatment with carbimazole has been stopped, regular checks need to be conducted, as the risk of relapse is highest in the first year after stopping treatment. If a relapse occurs, then radioactive iodine treatment or surgery may be required.

Radioactive Iodine

This is a one-off treatment where iodine which has a radioactive substance attached to it is introduced into the body orally. The iodine is taken up by the overactive parts of the gland, and the radioactive substance destroys the overactive cells. This treatment is performed once, and the patient is hospitalised and isolated for 24 hours, as they will be temporarily radioactive. It is recommended that a woman does not conceive for eight to twelve months following this treatment. The full effect of the procedure is seen after three months, and permanent hypothyroidism may occur. The success rate is about 80 per cent using this procedure, and it is the treatment of choice for multinodular goitre, or recurrent Graves' disease.

Thyroid Surgery

Partial removal of the thyroid gland is no longer a popular choice of treatment. Risks include damage to the vocal cords and the parathyroid gland, which lies very close to the thyroid gland and controls calcium levels in the body. Surgery is not performed during pregnancy or on patients where the gland is so enlarged that symptoms such as hoarseness and difficulty swallowing are a feature.

Goitre

Just a quick word on goitre. Goitre is a word which means enlargement of the thyroid gland. It is not a diagnosis, just a finding which is sometimes noticed by the patient but often goes undetected. It can be seen with normal thyroid function, hypothyroidism and hyperthyroidism. It can also be seen in whole populations where there is a general iodine deficiency in the soil of a geographical area. In Ireland, there are no iodine-deficient areas. All swellings in the neck area, whether from the thyroid gland or elsewhere, need to be checked out by your doctor.

Thyroid Cancer

Thyroid cancer is three times more common in women than in men. It is also more common in adults who had radiation treatment in their childhood. The thyroid gland is very susceptible to radiation, and is one of the more common cancers seen in people exposed to the effects of the Chernobyl disaster.

It usually presents as a lump in the thyroid gland itself, but swollen neck glands, voice changes or cough can also be seen. It can be difficult to spot a cancerous lump, so the only way to diagnose thyroid cancer is to take a small sample of the gland using a syringe or a biopsy. Treatment is usually through surgery, but other options can include chemotherapy and radiotherapy.

Key Points

- Hypothyroidism, or an underactive thyroid, is the most common thyroid problem, especially in older women.
- The symptoms of hypothyroidism are subtle and easy to miss, such as tiredness and poor energy levels.
- It is easily treated with thyroid hormone replacement, which usually needs to be life-long.
- Hyperthyroidism is a much less common condition but with more severe symptoms.
- Treatment of hyperthyroidism usually involves medication to block the overactive part of the gland, or surgery to remove it.

3

Cardiovascular Disease

It is not a particularly well-known fact that cardiovascular disease is the biggest health risk to women in Ireland. Women often fear breast cancer more, but their risk of cardiovascular disease is far higher. It is also much harder to spot the signs of heart disease in women, as they often display symptoms which are not typical of heart disease and can be easily mistaken for other complaints, such as shortness of breath and a general feeling of tiredness. This chapter is designed to briefly cover the main causes of cardiovascular disease, how to try and identify any risk factors you may have, and how to prevent it developing before irreversible damage is done.

What Is Cardiovascular Disease?

The term 'cardiovascular disease' includes all forms of heart and blood vessel disease. For the purposes of this chapter we are going to discuss the heart and blood vessels and how they can be adversely affected by various factors, leading to heart attack and stroke.

The lining of a blood vessel is supposed to be smooth and free from obstruction, to allow blood to be pumped easily and freely around the body. The lining can be affected in a variety of ways. With uncontrolled high blood pressure (hypertension), the lining is damaged by the increased pressure, becoming stiff and narrow. With high cholesterol levels (hypercholesterolaemia) cholesterol is deposited on the wall of the vessel; this is called plaque. The lining starts to thicken, and blood flow is no longer smooth. Eventually, this can lead to partial or total blockage of that vessel. This means that the part of the body beyond that blockage will be deprived of the oxygen and nutrients that it needs to survive, and this will lead to damage.

Atherosclerosis

Normal artery

Artery narrowed by atherosclerosis

Damage to or thickening of the blood vessel lining is known as 'atherosclerosis'. While atherosclerosis is developing you may have little or no symptoms. Eventually, however, a blood clot may form at an area of atherosclerosis in a vessel, which would cause a sudden and immediate blockage, leading to a stroke or heart attack.

Hypertension

Hypertension is the name given to high blood pressure. A 'normal' blood pressure reading is approximately 120/80 mmHg. While everyone's blood pressure reading is different, hypertension is when your blood pressure is consistently greater than 140/90 mmHg. Your blood pressure automatically increases as you get older, but for some it becomes high at a younger age and, if undetected, it can cause a lot of damage to blood vessels over the years, leading to a variety of health problems. It is recommended that you have your blood pressure checked every three years under the age of 40, and every year over the age of 40.

Symptoms and Causes of Hypertension

Hypertension usually causes no symptoms. When it is dangerously high, some may experience dizziness, headaches and nosebleeds.

Hypertension may occur for the following reasons:

- Being obese/overweight
- Smoking
- Having too much salt in your diet
- It runs in families
- Having an excessive alcohol intake
- Leading an inactive lifestyle
- As a result of certain diseases, such as diabetes or kidney disease
- Age or life stage: the older you are the more likely it is to develop. It is common in men in early middle age, but more common in women after the menopause.
- Race – it is more common in women of black origin than white.

Uncontrolled hypertension can lead to:

- Heart attack or stroke
- Aneurysm – a bulging in the wall of a blood vessel, which can cause it to burst suddenly

- Heart failure
- Eye disease and blindness
- Kidney disease and kidney failure

Diagnosis and Treatment of Hypertension

Sometimes when you go to the doctor, your blood pressure is higher because you may be a little anxious, so to diagnose true hypertension your doctor organises for you to wear a tape recorder and blood pressure cuff for 24 hours, during which time your blood pressure is recorded continuously. This is the best way to detect hypertension. Your doctor may also want to do some blood tests and an electrocardiography (ECG) to check your heart function.

Once hypertension has been confirmed, your doctor will start you on medication to lower it. There are many different types available, and sometimes two medications are needed to control it. It is very important that you continue to take your medication. Hypertension is usually not reversible (although in some cases medication can be stopped if you have lost a lot of weight), so lifelong treatment is usually needed to keep you well. If you are experiencing any side effects that are causing you to stop taking it, talk to your doctor about trying something different.

Apart from medication it is extremely important to change your lifestyle if you are diagnosed with hypertension; this involves eating healthier foods, losing weight if needed, reducing your salt intake, exercising more, reducing stress and alcohol intake and stopping smoking. It is also important to monitor your blood pressure readings at home with a monitor to ensure your hypertension remains well controlled.

Heart Attack (Myocardial Infarction)

Heart attacks are usually seen in women at a later age than men; this is thought to be because of the protective effect of oestrogen on the heart, which is not clearly understood. About ten years after the menopause, women catch up with men in terms of heart attack risk. However, a woman is more likely to die from a heart attack than a man, partially because the resultant muscle damage is often more extensive in women.

Causes of Heart Attacks

Heart attacks are caused by a blockage in the coronary arteries that supply blood to the heart muscle. This blockage is caused by athero-sclerosis of the coronary vessel walls. Angina is the name given to pain in the chest caused by reduced blood flow to the heart muscle. Angina is not a heart attack, but it means that you are much more likely to have a heart attack.

Symptoms of a Heart Attack

Women can experience symptoms that are quite different to those of men. This often leads to a misdiagnosis or delayed diagnosis, which accounts in part for the lower survival rate in women after a heart attack.

Symptoms to watch out for include:

- Chest pain or discomfort in the centre of your chest
- Shortness of breath
- Nausea and vomiting
- Feeling faint
- Sweating
- Heartburn
- Coughing
- Feeling tired
- Heart flutters
- Loss of appetite

As you can see from the last few symptoms, they are not what you would typically associate with a heart attack. If you are experiencing any of these symptoms you should go straight to your doctor or the closest casualty department. A delay in diagnosing a heart attack can mean the difference between life and death. Sudden death can occur because of a sudden change in the rhythm of the heart due to a lack of oxygen. If sufficient heart muscle has been damaged during the heart attack, the heart may not function properly in the long term, leading to chronic heart failure. The emergency management of a heart attack may include clot-busting drugs to break down the clot in the blood vessel, or the insertion of a stent within the vessel to reopen it, restoring vital blood flow.

Stroke

A stroke is the term given to the injury of brain tissue caused by an interruption of blood flow. There are a variety of ways that this happens, but atherosclerosis (damage to or thickening of the blood vessel lining) is the most common cause of a stroke. Strokes are a leading cause of death, but for survivors the loss of independence means that families often find themselves becoming carers. Financially, strokes are a huge burden on health care services, due to the high cost of providing long-term care for patients who have suffered severe strokes.

A stroke is a medical emergency. Just like a heart attack, the quicker you can be treated the more likely you are to recover, and less damage to the brain will occur. Some patients experience temporary symptoms of a stroke but then fully recover within 24 hours. This is called a transient ischaemic attack (TIA). This greatly increases your chances of having a full-blown stroke. A TIA should always be treated as a stroke, as there is no guarantee that normal function will return.

Symptoms of a Stroke

- Sudden onset of dizziness, unsteadiness and loss of balance
- Difficulty finding words or speaking
- Sudden onset of confusion
- Paralysis of one side of your body or face
- Difficulty seeing in one or both eyes
- Headache

Risk Factors for Heart Attack and Stroke

Cholesterol

Cholesterol is a fatty substance produced mostly by the liver and also taken in through your diet. A certain amount of cholesterol is required for the cells of the body to function. It is found in meat, poultry, fish and dairy products, but there is no cholesterol in plant products. The cholesterol absorbed from food is stored in the liver and released as needed.

LDL cholesterol (also known as 'bad cholesterol') is the form of cholesterol which is responsible for the formation of plaque in blood vessels. This leads to atherosclerosis, which in turn is responsible for heart disease and strokes.

HDL cholesterol ('good cholesterol') protects against atherosclerosis by removing cholesterol from the walls of blood vessels.

Therefore, high LDL and low HDL cholesterol levels are risk factors for atherosclerosis, while low LDL and high HDL cholesterol levels are protective against heart disease and stroke.

Preferred Cholesterol Levels

Type of cholesterol	Normal levels (mmol/L)
Total cholesterol	<5*
LDL cholesterol	<3
HDL cholesterol	>1

* Total cholesterol is the sum of HDL, LDL and other lipid components.

In some cases, extremely high levels of cholesterol in the blood can be due to a genetic disorder which runs in families. These families tend to have heart disease which develops at a younger age. Cholesterol levels can sometimes be managed with diet and exercise. A cholesterol-lowering diet is rich in nuts, seeds, fruit and vegetables, oily fish, oatmeal and wholegrains. If this doesn't work, a group of drugs known as statins are used. If statins are needed to control cholesterol levels, this is usually recommended as a permanent medication. About 20 per cent of statin users will experience marked side effects, such as muscular pains.

Hypertension

Hypertension or high blood pressure, if left uncontrolled for many years, will lead to stiffening of the wall of blood vessels. Plaque will then form on the damaged walls, leading to atherosclerosis. Blood pressure when treated with medication should be maintained below 140/85 mmHg.

Diabetes

It is well documented how poorly-controlled diabetes affects the tiny blood vessels in many organs, including the kidneys, skin and eyes. However, if you are a diabetic, you are also more likely to develop atherosclerosis in large vessels. Being diabetic gives you as high a chance of having heart disease as someone who has already had a heart attack.

Obesity

The risk of developing coronary artery disease and, therefore, having a heart attack is three to four times higher in women whose BMI is greater than 29.

Family History

Women with a family history of heart disease have an increased risk of heart attack. This is particularly true if the case of heart disease is in a male relative who is 55 or younger, or a female relative who is 65 or younger.

Smoking

Tobacco contains chemicals which cause blood vessel damage, leading to an increased risk of atherosclerosis.

Metabolic Syndrome

This is the name given to a group of conditions found in men and women which greatly increase a person's risk of developing cardiovascular disease and diabetes. Metabolic syndrome usually occurs with advancing age, although it is being detected more and more in younger people due to the obesity epidemic affecting our young people. The conditions that contribute to metabolic syndrome include:

- Increased blood pressure
- High blood sugar levels
- Excess body fat around the waist
- Abnormal cholesterol levels

If you have three of these conditions, you have metabolic syndrome, or Syndrome X as it is also known. We know that having any one of these conditions increases your risk of heart attack and stroke, but if you have three or more your risk is even greater.

Symptoms and Treatment

You will not experience any symptoms when you have metabolic syndrome. The concept of identifying patients with metabolic syndrome is to detect women who are at a high risk of developing significant illnesses such as heart disease, stroke, diabetes and hypertension. If the patient changes her lifestyle, these illnesses can be avoided to a large extent, improving the woman's quality of life.

These changes need to include:

- Stopping smoking
- Regular exercise, such as 30 to 60 minutes of brisk walking daily
- Weight loss – the loss of between 5 and 10 per cent of your total body weight can be enough to return glucose levels and blood pressure to normal.
- A healthy eating plan – a Mediterranean-type diet has been shown to be particularly good for the metabolic syndrome patient, with the emphasis on fruit, vegetables, healthy fats, fish and wholegrains.

If your goals cannot be achieved with lifestyle changes alone, your doctor may need to add in medication to lower blood pressure, control cholesterol or help you lose weight.

Key Points

- Cardiovascular disease is the biggest cause of death in women every year in Ireland.
- Hormones protect women until the menopause, and then the risk of cardiovascular disease starts to increase.
- The symptoms of a heart attack in women can be unusual.
- Factors that increase your risk of cardiovascular disease are high cholesterol, high blood pressure, diabetes, obesity and smoking.
- Having metabolic syndrome means you are more likely to develop cardiovascular disease if you do not change your lifestyle.

4

Benign Breast Problems

Most women will have met or know of another woman who has had breast cancer, and this sometimes leads to a fear of developing breast cancer. The good news is that it also means that a woman is far more likely to see a doctor to get a breast cancer symptom checked out for reassurance. About half of all visits regarding breast symptoms are because of either breast pain or a breast lump. Breast symptom complaints are seen most commonly in the 25 to 44-year-old age group, and in the over 65 age group. If you are worried get it checked, but the main thing to remember is that most breast lumps are benign (non-cancerous).

Benign Breast Lumps

There are several types of benign breast lumps, the most common of which are discussed in more detail below.

Fibroadenoma

This is a usually a small, firm, rubbery lump, which moves easily under your fingertips when examined. It is the most common breast lump found in women aged under 30. Up to 15 per cent of women can have more than one of these lumps. They tend to grow in response to hormones, and often change in size at puberty, during menstrual cycles, pregnancy and breastfeeding. They tend to shrink after the menopause. Once a lump has been identified as a fibroadenoma it is usually just watched and not surgically removed. Exceptions to this include situations where the lump is changing the shape of the breast, causing pain or discomfort, or if the patient is very concerned about the presence of the lump and would like it removed.

Fibrocystic Breast Disease

This is now considered to be a normal condition which causes lumpiness and pain or discomfort for women, usually premenstrually, but it can occur at other times during the menstrual cycle. It is most commonly seen in women aged over 30, particularly when hormone production becomes a bit more erratic and the menstrual cycle is becoming more irregular. It is usually found in both breasts, but one breast can be more symptomatic than the other. Most women will experience symptoms of this in the upper, outer quadrant of the breast, i.e. the part of the breast closest to the armpit. Fibrocystic breast disease is extremely common, with up to 60 per cent of all women experiencing it at some time or another. It is controlled by the same hormones that control the menstrual cycle – oestrogen and progesterone. The breasts are preparing for pregnancy in the second half of the menstrual cycle, so the milk-producing glands increase in size and number. This can cause pain and swelling. When the period occurs, the increased number of cells is slowly killed off in a natural process, but it can lead to scarring or fibrosis, which causes the lumpy feeling felt on examination.

Breast Cysts

A breast cyst is a fluid-filled sac found within breast tissue. It can occur anywhere within the breast. A cyst causes swelling in the breast, which may or may not cause associated pain. It tends to be influenced by hormone production and can often change in size according to the menstrual cycle. If the cyst develops quickly during a menstrual cycle it is more likely to cause pain. Breast cysts are more commonly seen in women over 40. They are not usually seen in postmenopausal women, unless they are taking hormone replacement therapy (HRT).

Fat Necrosis

This is an area of inflammation within the fat of the breast tissue, which can happen due to a range of causes, including accidental trauma, breast surgeries (such as a breast reduction or implant removal) and radiotherapy. It can cause a lump which can be quite hard when felt but is harmless.

How Do I Find Out What the Breast Lump Is?

Breast lumps are investigated using 'triple assessment':

1. Examination by a breast specialist – often the specialist will have a very good idea of exactly what the lump is before the other investigations are done.
2. Mammography and/or breast ultrasound – depending on the nature of the lump and the woman's age, either of these investigations may be required. Ultrasound is very helpful if a tissue sample is needed or if a cyst is to be drained.
3. Fine needle aspiration/breast lump biopsy – if the lump is thought to be benign, fine needle aspiration is usually done. This involves placing a needle into the breast lump under the guidance of ultrasound, and cells can be sucked back or 'aspirated' into the syringe, along with any fluid from within the lump. This sample is then sent for examination to confirm the diagnosis.

Treatment of Benign Breast Lumps

Luckily, the overwhelming majority of breast lumps turn out to be benign. Reassurance may be sufficient for some women if their examination is normal and no lump is felt. Other treatment options vary according to the type of breast lump:

- In the case of fibroadenoma, the lump can usually be left alone or removed if the patient is worried about it or it increases in size.
- For fibrocystic breast disease, treatment consists of practical advice, such as wearing a firm control bra, using a sports bra for exercise or in bed if pain is a big issue, use of evening primrose oil or vitamin B6 capsules, reducing caffeine intake, and in some cases where the symptoms are very severe premenstrually, using the combined oral contraceptive pill.
- For cysts, aspiration or sucking out of the fluid within the cyst usually relieves the pain and swelling instantly.
- If fat necrosis has happened recently, then applying a hot cloth to the area may help to let it settle naturally over time. If it is a long-standing problem and is causing a lot of pain, it may be appropriate to remove the lump.

Breast Pain

Breast pain (mastalgia) can either be cyclical, for example related to some time within your menstrual cycle, or non-cyclical, meaning it can occur randomly at any time. It is much more commonly seen in premenopausal women than in women who have gone through the menopause. This is probably because, although we are not really sure why breast pain happens, it is thought to be related to increased hormone levels during the menstrual cycle. Occasionally in older women a benign cause, like a cyst or a lump, is found to be the source of the pain. It is rarely a symptom of breast cancer.

Cyclical breast pain is usually felt throughout both breasts, and can extend up into the armpits. It is described as a heaviness or a dull ache. It usually improves greatly after the period and requires no treatment, resolving spontaneously.

Older women in the 40 to 50 age group are more likely to have a sharp pain in one breast, and in quite a specific area. There is no relationship with the menstrual cycle. Occasionally, a lump can be identified in the area of pain.

When being treated for breast pain, your doctor should ask you some relevant questions, in particular about your menstrual cycle and any irregularity in it, any recent emotional stress, or any change in medications. Breast examination findings are usually completely normal, and in younger women no further investigations are needed. In older women whose pain is confined to one small area a mammogram is probably a good idea, even if the examination results are normal.

Treatment of Breast Pain

First, it is important to say that the majority of younger women with cyclical breast pain will find that it improves over time. You will get better without any treatment or help. It is helpful for your doctor if you can keep a diary over one month of breast pain and the severity of it on different days, so that your doctor can get an idea of how bad it is and for how many days you are affected by it.

The following treatments have been used for breast pain with varying results:

- Vitamin E has been shown by some studies to improve symptoms.
- Evening primrose oil has been shown to improve mastalgia symptoms.

- Reducing caffeine intake; there is no evidence that this works.
- Vitamin B6 has mixed results; some studies show it works, others don't.

If a cause is found for the breast pain, such as a cyst or lump, then surgery can help with the pain. Surgery is not useful when there is no lump. In rare cases where breast pain is very debilitating a drug called Danazol is used with good results. However, 20 per cent of patients will experience quite marked menstrual irregularity, acne and excessive facial hair when taking this drug, so it is not commonly used.

Nipple Discharge

The presence of a discharge from the nipple is not cancerous in the vast majority of women; however, it often causes great concern when it is seen. There are three main types of discharge:

1. Milk – this is seen in women for lots of different reasons. For example, for up to two years after finishing breastfeeding a child, a milky discharge is normal. Other reasons include nipple stimulation, certain medications and some hormonal syndromes which usually involve an absence of periods.
2. Abnormal but no underlying problem – the discharge here is usually from both breasts and can only be seen when the nipple is being squeezed. The discharge comes from several ducts on the surface of the nipple, and the colour can range from clear, white, yellow through to dark green.
3. Abnormal but possible underlying problem – this type of discharge is usually from one breast, is spontaneously seen without having to squeeze the nipple, and is blood-stained.

A full breast examination to assess any underlying lumps in the breasts should be carried out, and a mammogram should be performed on older women with a nipple discharge. If the results of the examination and mammogram are normal, women should be advised to avoid any stimulation of the nipple, and eventually the discharge should disappear.

If the discharge is coming from one breast and is blood-stained, then you should be referred to a breast surgeon. The most common causes of this type of discharge are two benign causes – intraductal papilloma or duct ectasia – and surgery to remove the underlying cause may be a good option. A blood-stained discharge with a breast lump increases the risk of breast cancer.

Inverted Nipples

Inverted nipples affect about 3 per cent of women. Most inverted nipples are congenital. That means that you are born with both nipples pointing inwards to some degree. A new appearance of an inverted nipple should always be investigated, as it can be a sign of an underlying cancer.

There are three grades of inverted nipples:

- Grade 1 – the nipple can be everted or made to point outwards with either stimulation or cold. The nipple usually stays everted for some time and then retracts.
- Grade 2 – the nipple is difficult to evert and never stays everted for long.
- Grade 3 – the nipple is severely inverted and can never be made to evert.

Nipple inversion is only a concern with breastfeeding when it is grade 2 or 3. Usually, with the exception of breastfeeding, inverted nipples cause no problems. However, particularly in some younger women, the appearance of inverted nipples can cause a lot of psychological distress, and they may benefit from cosmetic surgery to evert the nipples.

Tuberous Breasts

This is a condition that women are born with, also known as a congenital condition. The breast tissue itself does not develop during puberty, and the breast becomes a specific shape. This includes quite a large areola, which is the circular, darker skin around the nipple, which points outwards from the chest wall. There is little breast tissue itself behind the areola. Women can have anything ranging from mild to severe forms of this. In its more severe form breast-feeding can be difficult, as there is very little milk-producing tissue. Some women will opt for breast enlargement with implants, which corrects the appearance quite dramatically.

Breast Infections

Breast infection is a common complaint and can include mastitis and breast abscesses. Infection is mostly seen in breastfeeding women, but mastitis can occur in women who are not breastfeeding and, indeed, in postmenopausal women. Mastitis is most commonly seen one to three months after the birth of a baby. It is caused by the introduction of bacteria into the breast tissue, usually from the baby's mouth. Invariably there is a crack in the surface of the nipple in breastfeeding women, and that is the source of infection.

Symptoms include pain, redness, fever, nausea, aches and shivering. There may be an area of redness visible on the breast skin.

It is very important for breastfeeding women to continue to feed from the infected breast. There is no risk at all to the baby, and if feeding from the sore breast is reduced or stopped the breast will become engorged with milk and the pain and swelling will increase. If breastfeeding is not possible, then expressing milk by hand or with a pump is advisable.

Frequent feeds from the affected breast are often enough to settle the mastitis, and if symptoms are improving you can just keep an eye on it. However, if you have a persistently high temperature of over 38.5°C and you are feeling unwell, it is likely that you will need antibiotics from your doctor.

Sometimes mastitis can develop into a breast abscess. This is a collection of pus within the breast. It is characterised by an extremely tender lump within the breast, failure to improve despite a few days of antibiotics, or pus discharging from the nipple. This is treated with surgery to open up the lump which has formed and to drain the pus from the breast. Antibiotics are then required after surgery.

Mastitis and breast abscesses are much less commonly seen in non-breastfeeding women, but they do occur. Mastitis can be associated with a form of breast cancer, so always get your breast checked if you have any unusual symptoms.

Breast Self-examination

Experts tell us that regular monthly breast self-examination (BSE) does not reduce the numbers of women who die from breast cancer. The stress and anxiety that women have to endure when they find a breast lump (which almost always turns out to be benign) does not appear to improve the long-term outcome for women who do end up having breast cancer. However, we know that most breast cancers are detected by women themselves. The best advice to women is to know what is normal for you, and that can only happen if you are aware of your own breasts. Then you will always know when something new has developed, and you should talk to your doctor about the breast change.

Below is a simple guide to examining your breasts. If you are having periods, it is best to examine your breasts one week after the start of the period, when they are least likely to be tender or enlarged due to hormonal changes.

Breast Self-examination

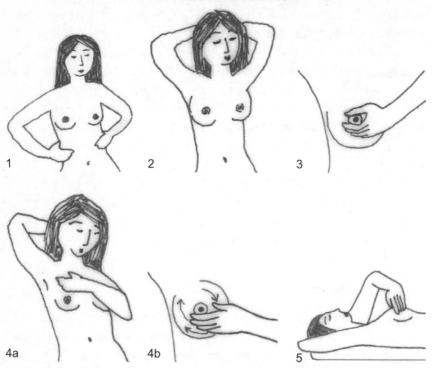

Breast Self-examination (BSE) Procedure

1. Stand in front of the mirror with no clothes on from the waist up, with your hands on your hips. Look at the shape of the breasts, the overlying skin and the nipples.
2. Raise your arms above your head and look at the breasts again.
3. Check for any nipple discharge from either nipple.
4. Stand either in the shower or in front of the mirror and examine your left breast with your right hand. Keeping your hand flat against your chest, use your middle three fingers to examine the breast using a circular motion the size of a two-euro coin, while keeping the three fingers together and flat. Make sure you cover the full extent of the breast; this includes from the armpit to the cleavage

and from the collar bone to the top of the abdomen. Repeat this procedure by examining the right breast with your left hand.
5. Repeat step 4 while lying down flat.

Key Points

- Most breast lumps are not cancerous.
- Breast lumps are investigated using mammogram, ultrasound and sampling of the lump if necessary.
- Breast lumps are often left untreated unless they are causing a lot of symptoms, such as pain.
- Blood-stained nipple discharge always needs investigation.
- Mastalgia usually resolves over time.

5

Female Cancers

In the past, there has been a tendency to avoid the subject of cancer – the big C – but the truth is that the incidence of cancer in women is on the rise. This is partly to do with our lifestyle choices, but also because of the increased life expectancy of Irish women. The older we get, the more likely we are to develop a cancer of some kind. Over two-thirds of cancers occur in the over 65 age group. As a nation we have a high cancer incidence – the second-highest in Europe. If you look at Irish women of all ages as a group, we have a one-in-four lifetime risk of getting cancer. So, with statistics like these, it is extremely important that we understand the symptoms and signs of early cancer and, most importantly, concentrate on what we can do as individuals to reduce our risk of cancers by understanding how they can arise.

The Most Common Cancers in Irish Women

- Non-melanoma skin cancer – 29 per cent
- Breast cancer – 23 per cent
- Bowel cancer – 8 per cent
- Lung cancer – 7 per cent
- Melanoma – 3 per cent
- Gynaecological:
  - Uterine cancer – 3 per cent

○ Ovarian cancer – 3 per cent
○ Cervical cancer – 2 per cent

Non-melanoma Skin Cancers

This group of cancers includes the most common cancers in the western world. The main cancers are basal cell carcinoma (BCC) and squamous cell carcinoma (SCC). BCC is much more common than SCC, but they have a lot of similarities. They are both associated with light-coloured skin and too much sun exposure and, therefore, are found on skin which may be exposed to the sun for long periods, such as the face, scalp, ears, hands, and so on.

BCC is a very slow-growing skin cancer which accounts for 75 per cent of all skin cancers. It is usually seen in women with fair skin and is found in areas that have had a lot of sun exposure. It usually spreads only superficially, but this spread, if not caught early, can cause a lot of local damage, especially on the face. BCC usually presents as a raised pink or pearly-white lump with rolled edges. SCC is less common and usually presents as a growing bump with a scaly surface and reddish patches.

Diagnosis of Non-melanoma Skin Cancers

Skin cancer is diagnosed through a biopsy of the abnormal-looking area, which means taking a small sample of the abnormal skin for careful examination.

Symptoms of Non-melanoma Skin Cancers

Signs and symptoms to watch out for include:

- A new pink or pearly-white area of skin
- An area of skin which is not healing well or oozing for a while, or crusting over repeatedly

- An area which bleeds easily
- An ulcer or growing bump with red scaly patches
- An area with small, irregular blood vessels around it

Treatment Options

Treatment of non-melanoma skin cancer depends on the size, depth and location of the cancer. Treatment options include:

- Excision or cutting out of the skin cancer and closing it with stitches
- Curettage and electrodessication, i.e. scraping away the lesion and using electricity to burn off any remaining cancer cells; this is suitable only for cancers which are not deep.
- Mohs surgery, where small pieces of skin are removed and immediately examined; the process is repeated until no more cancer cells are seen.
- Radiation is sometimes required if the cancer has spread to other areas of the body.
- Creams may be applied to the cancerous areas, such as 5 fluorouracil (5FU) or Imiquimod can be used to treat superficial cancers.

Most non-melanoma skin cancers do not recur, although this depends on the size of the original skin cancer.

Breast Cancer

One in eight women will develop breast cancer in their lifetime. Most of us know, or know of, someone who has had breast cancer. Irish women have a high risk of developing breast cancer compared with other European women – the fourth highest rate in Europe.

The majority of breast cancers start in the milk ducts of the breast, and are known as ductal carcinomas. A minority of breast cancers arise in the milk-producing lobules of the breast tissue.

Risk Factors for Developing Breast Cancer

There are a lot of risk factors for breast cancer that are beyond our control, but there are some that we can definitely try to influence to reduce our risk. The risk factors include:

- Being female
- Obesity
- Increasing age – your risk of breast cancer increases as you age. Women over the age of 55 have a greater risk than younger women.
- Previous instance of breast cancer – if you have had breast cancer in one breast, you have an increased risk of developing cancer in your other breast.
- A family history of breast cancer – if you have a mother, sister or daughter with breast cancer, your risk of being diagnosed with breast cancer doubles.
- Inherited genes that increase cancer – the most common genes that increase your risk of developing breast and other cancers are BRCA1 and BRCA2. In order for cancer to start in a breast cell, the genes of that cell need to be damaged (or mutated) several times. However, in a breast cell which contains the BRCA1 OR BRCA2 gene, some mutations have already happened, so less damage needs to occur to that cell to turn it into a breast cancer cell.
- Radiation exposure – if you received radiation treatments to your chest as a child or young adult you are more likely to develop breast cancer later in life.
- Beginning your period at a younger age – beginning your period before the age of 12 increases your risk of breast

cancer. This is thought to be as a result of being exposed to female hormones for a longer period over your lifetime.

- Beginning menopause at an older age – if you begin the menopause after the age of 55, you are more likely to develop breast cancer. This is also thought to be as a result of being exposed to female hormones for a longer period over your lifetime.
- Having your first child at an older age – women who give birth to their first child after the age of 35 may have an increased risk of breast cancer. This is because pregnancy matures breast cells and makes them more stable, and less susceptible to cancer changes caused by female hormones.
- Undergoing postmenopausal hormone therapy for longer than five to seven years – women who take hormone therapy medications that combine oestrogen and progesterone to treat the signs and symptoms of menopause have an increased risk of breast cancer after continuous use for more than five to seven years.
- Drinking alcohol increases the risk of developing breast cancer.
- Breastfeeding for prolonged periods may *reduce* your risk of breast cancer.

Inherited Breast Cancer

Only about 5 per cent of all breast cancers are due to an inherited genetic problem. Two main genetic defects, called BRCA1 and BRCA2, greatly increase your risk of developing breast and ovarian cancer if present. If you have a very strong family history of breast cancer or other cancers you should talk to your doctor about taking a blood test to see if you have the abnormal gene. Counselling is required before undergoing the test, as there are significant implications for you if you obtain a positive result for the presence of these abnormalities. These tests are very useful for detecting if you are at high risk, but they cannot identify who will definitely develop cancer in the future.

Symptoms of Breast Cancer

The following are changes to watch out for:

- A lump or thickness in a breast which hasn't previously been present
- Nipple changes, such as a newly-inverted nipple
- Skin changes, such as dimpling or redness and scaling
- Bloody discharge from a nipple
- Breast abscess
- Any change in the size or shape of a breast

Tests and Diagnosis

Examination

Your doctor will examine both breasts to detect any abnormal lump. This may be done while you are lying and sitting, and with your arms by your side and above your head. Your doctor will also examine your armpits to feel for enlarged lymph glands.

Mammogram

This x-ray of the breast is also used when screening for breast cancer in women with no symptoms. However, if a lump has been found, a mammogram can be helpful.

Ultrasound

This test is useful for determining whether a breast lump is solid or filled with fluid, and can give more information as to whether the lump looks like cancer. Also, if a sample of the lump is required, this is done under the guidance of ultrasound to ensure a proper sample of the lump is obtained.

Biopsy

This enables laboratory technicians to examine cells from the lump under a microscope to give a definite diagnosis of cancer.

MRI

This determines the extent of the cancer and whether your other breast is healthy. This information is very useful before having surgery.

As part of your overall breast cancer treatment, the cancer needs to be staged. This means to establish whether there has been any spread outside the breast to other organs. Stages range from 0 to IV. Stage 0 is when the breast cancer is very small and not invasive; stage IV is when the cancer has spread to other areas in the body. Staging determines what type of treatment is most appropriate to you, and also helps to decide the length of treatment to some extent. Sometimes a full picture of the stage of your disease is not available until after surgery. Some tests which may be ordered for staging include:

- Bone scan
- Chest x-ray
- CT scan/MRI
- Mammogram and MRI of the other breast

Treatment of Breast Cancer

The treatment options available include:

- A lumpectomy, or the removal of the breast cancer. The surgeon removes only the lump and some surrounding normal breast tissue. This is only suitable for some small lumps.
- A mastectomy, or removal of the breast. This can be a simple mastectomy, where just the breast tissue is removed

completely. In some unusual cases, a radical mastectomy is needed, where the underlying muscle is also removed.

- The removal of one lymph gland from the axilla or armpit on the affected side – this is also known as sentinel node sampling. The surgeon picks one lymph gland which is the most likely to contain cancer cells. If there is no cancer in it, it is very unlikely that the cancer has spread to the armpit, and the rest of the lymph glands are left in place.
- The removal of several lymph glands – also known as axillary node dissection. This is done when the sentinel node contains cancer cells. It is sometimes avoided by using radiotherapy, as there are permanent side effects associated with removal of the lymph glands, such as long-term swelling and discomfort in the affected arm.
- Radiotherapy, which is a high-energy beam, similar to an x-ray. It is directed onto the area of skin overlying the cancer to kill off cancer cells that may be remaining in the area. It is used in early stage breast cancer, and is also used when the cancer is large in size.
- Chemotherapy, which uses toxic drugs to kill off cancer cells, and is usually given through a vein but can also be in tablet form. It is used after surgery, or before surgery to shrink a particularly large cancer. Side effects include hair loss, nausea, vomiting and tiredness.
- Hormone therapy, which involves employing a group of drugs that aim to block hormones acting in the body to prevent any further stimulation of cancer cells by hormones produced naturally within the female body. These drugs include the following:
  ◦ Tamoxifen, which is probably the best-known breast cancer drug. This stops oestrogen from attaching to the cancer cell, thus stopping it from growing.

- ○ Arimidex, which is used only in women who develop breast cancer postmenopausally. It stops androgens from being converted to oestrogen.
- ○ Herceptin, which blocks the production of a protein called HER2, which feeds cancer cells and helps them grow.
- Surgery to remove the ovaries in a premenopausal woman may be necessary in some cases. This causes what is called a surgical menopause.

The success of treatment for breast cancer is measured in the percentage of women who are alive five years after being diagnosed with the disease. At present, the average five-year survival rate is 80 per cent, and this is increasing all the time. This is due to increasingly early detection, breast cancer screening through mammograms and advances in treatments. This figure of 80 per cent will certainly increase again as more innovative treatments are developed, and as clinical trials give us more information on how best to treat breast cancer. The message to remember is this: cancer is something that you can survive, but early detection is the key. So if you are worried about anything related to your breasts go and see your doctor as soon as possible.

Cervical Cancer

Cervical cancer may not be one of the more common female cancers overall, but it is the second most common cancer — after breast cancer — among the 15 to 44-year-old age group. The peak age range for the incidence of cervical cancer is 35 to 47 years.

Cervical Cancer and the Human Papillomavirus (HPV)

Recently it has been proven that there is a direct link between cervical cancer and the human papillomavirus (HPV). Over 85 per cent of cases of invasive cervical cancer are caused by this virus.

HPV is a sexually-transmitted disease which is easily spread among sexual partners. It is spread through genital skin contact; in other words, it can be transmitted from person to person without penetrative sex. For the majority of women it remains in the genital area for three to five years, and it is estimated that, at any given time, approximately 11 per cent of the general female population has HPV detectable in their cervix. After that time period the immune system will usually fight the virus and eventually remove it from the body.

During this period the woman usually has no idea that she is infected and has no symptoms. However, in some cases the virus will cause problems, either appearing as genital warts (see Chapter 7) or causing routine cervical smears to become abnormal.

There are numerous types of HPV: some cause warts (types 6 and 11), while others cause precancerous cell changes which can be detected in a cervical smear test (types 16 and 18). The length of time between becoming infected with HPV and developing warts or precancerous cell changes in smears varies enormously from woman to woman. It can be many years between the two. This can lead to questions being asked about fidelity and other sexual partners, so it is important that this can be explained to the partner concerned.

In a small number of women, HPV will remain in the genital area, leading to persistent smear problems, which may get slowly worse over time.

Risk Factors for Developing Cervical Cancer

Factors that will increase your risk of developing cervical cancer include:

- HPV infection
- Smoking
- A lack of, or very infrequent, cervical smears

- HIV and other states of chronic immunosuppression, such as with organ transplant patients
- Exposure to diethylstilboestrol (DES) also increases cervical cancer risk. DES is a drug that was given to pregnant women in the 1960s to prevent miscarriage and premature labour. It is now known to cause the daughters of women given the drug to have a higher risk of cervical, breast and vaginal cancer.

Symptoms of Cervical Cancer

Unfortunately, cervical cancer has few symptoms or signs until it has reached an advanced stage. Early cervical cancer has no symptoms, and the cervix appears normal on examination. Any abnormalities will only be identified by smear examination.

Some symptoms associated with cervical cancer include:

- Abnormal vaginal bleeding, either spontaneously or after sex
- Pain with sex
- Bloody vaginal discharge
- Pelvic pain

Diagnosis and Tests

A full medical history and examination by the doctor should be done. A speculum examination (similar to when you have a smear) may show the doctor that the cervix does not look normal, and the cervix may bleed easily when touched. A smear should be taken, or if the doctor is sure that the cervix is abnormal, they may refer you directly for a colposcopy procedure. This is an outpatient procedure in the gynaecology department of your local hospital. It involves putting a speculum into the vagina, similar to a smear, but a microscope is then focused on the cervix. This allows close inspection of the cervix and any abnormal-looking area is biopsied. Colposcopy is not painful, and no anaesthetic is needed.

If the smear indicates cervical cancer, then a colposcopy is done to confirm the presence of invasive cancer. Likewise, any suspicious lesion on the cervix is also biopsied. Once cancer has been confirmed, the extent of the cancer needs to be established, as this decides the most appropriate form of treatment. This involves looking at other organs of the body that lie close to the cervix, such as the colon and bladder, as well as organs that lie further away, such as the lungs.

Cervical cancer which is detected early is more suitable for surgery, whereas more advanced cancer usually needs radiotherapy and chemotherapy.

Abnormal Smears

Cervical smears involve taking a sample of cells using a soft brush from the neck of the womb, or cervix. These cells are then examined under the microscope for any changes. It is important to understand the significance of your smear result, so that you can put it in perspective. For some women a mildly abnormal smear result may be devastating and a constant source of worry, whereas in fact there is no real need for concern if the test is closely followed up. For other women the importance of repeating the smear in six months if it is mildly abnormal may not be stressed sufficiently, and they may not bother to return for a follow up.

The following are all the possible results of a smear test which you may encounter, and their significance:

Borderline Nuclear Abnormality (BNA)

This is the least abnormal result you can have in a smear. This has a 60 to 70 per cent chance of going back to normal spontaneously without any treatment. However, if this is persistently present in three consecutive smears over eighteen months, it is recommended to refer the patient for colposcopy.

Cervical Intraepithelial Neoplasia Grade 1 (CIN 1)

CIN1 is also known as low grade squamous intraepithelial lesion (LSIL). This is the next stage up from BNA. The abnormality seen in the smear is still classed as minor, and the smear is repeated six months later. If the CIN 1 remains at this time, then colposcopy is done. If the abnormality has improved and gone to BNA or normal, then another smear should be done six months later.

CIN 2/CIN 3

This level of smear abnormality, which is also known as high grade squamous intraepithelial lesion (HSIL), needs to be examined with a colposcopy within a few weeks of the smear result. The smear may not be accurate, and colposcopy may show that the abnormality has been overestimated. If the smear result is correct, a long loop excision of the transitional zone (LLETZ) procedure is done. This is a small wire loop heated to a high temperature which removes the part of the cervix that contains the abnormal cells. This is done at the same time as colposcopy, and no anaesthetic is required, as the cervix has no nerve supply. This procedure permanently removes the cervix abnormality in 95 per cent of cases. In the remaining 5 per cent of cases, a repeat LLETZ is required.

Cervical Cancer Screening

Compared to a lot of other cancers, cervical cancer has a lower survival rate. This is because it is a silent cancer, with symptoms only appearing at a relatively late stage. This is exactly the reason why a test which detects the early stages before it actually turns into cancer is so important. Not many cancers have such a test, but with cervical cancer we are lucky enough to have one.

The average age for the development of abnormal smears is between 25 and 35 and, therefore, to start a cervical screening programme in this age group greatly increases the chances of detecting it early and preventing full-blown cancer from developing. The National Cervical Screening Programme, known as Cervical-Check, has been in existence since September 2008 and hopes to reduce cervical cancer by 80 per cent. All women over the age of 25 are invited to have a free cervical smear with a registered smear taker, and the smear is repeated every three years. Often, women are concerned about having a smear only once every three years. However, the way cervical changes occur is very well understood; it is a slow process, and invasive cervical cancer does not arise in women within a three-year interval between smears.

Vaccination Against Cervical Cancer

The cervical cancer vaccine has recently been developed, specifically to protect against HPV. It is intended to be administered to girls before they first become sexually active, but that is not a requirement for vaccination.

The vaccine is administered over a six-month period, with three vaccinations at zero, two and six months. There are very few known side effects associated with the vaccine. Based on the information so far, the vaccine confers almost 100 per cent protection against HPV. Gardasil, which is the vaccine used in the national vaccination programme for 12-year-old girls in Ireland, also provides 100 per cent protection against HPV 6 and 11, which are responsible for 90 per cent of genital warts. It is still recommended that vaccinated women continue to have cervical smears on a regular basis.

Ovarian Cancer

Ovarian cancer is most common in women after the menopause, although it can affect women of all ages. The most common type of ovarian cancer is that of the outside layer of cells, known as epithelial cancer.

The symptoms of ovarian cancer are often mistaken for other conditions, such as irritable bowel syndrome (IBS). Typical symptoms of ovarian cancer include:

- Persistent abdominal or pelvic pain
- Pelvic pressure
- Bloating that is constant (i.e. not related to eating, as with IBS)
- Feeling of fullness

Risk Factors and Causes of Ovarian Cancer

- Being postmenopausal, in particular being over the age of 65, increases your risk of developing ovarian cancer.
- We know that being on the pill, having pregnancies and breastfeeding protects against ovarian cancer. This is because you are not releasing an egg every month under these conditions. It is thought that releasing an egg month after month for your reproductive life can increase the chances of ovarian cells turning cancerous. It is also suggested that multiple fertility treatments can increase your risk of ovarian cancer for the same reason, although this has not been proven.
- Approximately 10 per cent of ovarian cancers are due to an inherited faulty gene. Having a close relative with ovarian cancer, such as a sister, mother or daughter, increases your risk of developing ovarian cancer. If there is both ovarian cancer and breast cancer in close female relatives it may be appropriate to test for the BRCA1 and BRCA2 genes (see the section on breast cancer above).
- Endometriosis, a benign disease of the pelvis, where endometrium (womb lining) is found in areas outside the womb, and most commonly on the ovaries, may increase your chances of ovarian cancer.

Diagnosis and Tests

Your doctor will take a history of your symptoms and perform an abdominal examination as well as a pelvic examination. You may be referred directly to a specialist for investigations or your doctor may order some tests first. These include:

- A blood test – a chemical called CA 125 is released by ovarian cancers, and this can be detected by a simple blood test. However, some early cancers do not produce CA 125 in abnormally high amounts, and there are other non-cancer reasons for having a raised level of CA 125.
- An ultrasound – this allows the doctor to get a good view of your ovaries.

Treatment of Ovarian Cancer

If you have been diagnosed with ovarian cancer, the next step is to check out the rest of your body to see how advanced the cancer is. This helps the specialist to decide on the best form of treatment for you. Further tests may include:

- Chest x-ray
- MRI/CT scan of your chest/abdomen
- If there is any fluid inside your abdomen from the cancer which may have been causing the bloating, then the doctor may want to get a sample of this by passing a needle into your abdomen to take a sample of fluid. This is then checked for cancer cells.

Treatment for ovarian cancer usually involves surgery to remove the womb, ovaries, tubes and a layer of fat called the omentum, which lies inside the abdominal cavity. Chemotherapy is then sometimes performed after surgery.

Screening for Ovarian Cancer

Unfortunately, there is no screening test, like a cervical smear, that will detect early ovarian cancer. However, a combination of a test for the levels of the chemical CA 125 and a transvaginal ultrasound can be offered annually to women who are considered to be at increased risk due to their family history. This is usually started five years before the youngest affected family member was diagnosed; for example, if your sister was diagnosed with ovarian cancer at the age of 55, it is suggested that you start being screened annually from the age of 50 onwards.

Uterine Cancer (Cancer of the Womb)

This is also known as endometrial cancer, as the cancer occurs in the cells which line the womb, called the endometrium. The endometrium bleeds monthly, known as a 'period'. In over 90 per cent of cases, this cancer is seen in postmenopausal women.

Risk Factors for Uterine Cancer

There are a few reasons why uterine cancer is more likely to occur in some women. These include:

- Age – the risk of uterine cancer increases with age.
- Obesity – women with too much body fat have higher levels of oestrogen in their bodies. If you are overweight, your risk is increased threefold. If your BMI is 40, your risk of getting uterine cancer is increased sixfold.
- Presence of oestrogen – the hormone stimulates the endometrium, and when not properly balanced by progesterone, this can lead to uterine cancer.
- HRT – the two hormones used in HRT are oestrogen and progestogen; if these are not balanced properly it can lead

to overstimulation of the endometrium, which increases the cancer risk.

- Polycystic ovarian syndrome (PCOS) – in PCOS, oestrogen production can be unbalanced, leading to over-thickening of the endometrium. If left untreated over a long period of time the risk of uterine cancer increases.
- Tamoxifen – this drug used in the prevention of recurrent breast cancer slightly increases a woman's risk of developing uterine cancer. However, its beneficial effect in treating breast cancer greatly outweighs its relatively small risk of causing uterine cancer.
- In women who have never been pregnant the risk of developing uterine cancer is higher. It is thought that, like ovarian cancer, the hormones associated with pregnancy are protective against the cancer in later life.

Symptoms of Uterine Cancer

The main symptom of uterine cancer is abnormal bleeding. In women who are postmenopausal this is an easy symptom to spot, and usually they contact their doctor quickly. In women who are still having periods, their periods may get heavier, or they may experience bleeding between their normal periods. In more advanced uterine cancer the patient may experience lower back pain or weight loss. It is important to remember that only 10 per cent of postmenopausal women who experience bleeding will have uterine cancer.

Diagnosis and Treatment

Uterine cancer is diagnosed usually on ultrasound, where the endometrium is found to be thicker than normal. A biopsy is taken which confirms the diagnosis, and various tests are used to determine the extent of the cancer, including a CT scan, MRI, chest x-ray and blood tests.

Treatment usually involves surgery to remove the womb, ovaries and fallopian tubes, and possibly chemotherapy and/or radiotherapy if needed.

Colon (Bowel) Cancer

The bowel is the long tube inside the abdomen that is responsible for the filtering of our food, and is divided into the small bowel and the large bowel. The small bowel is much less commonly affected by cancer. Therefore, this section relates only to the large bowel.

The function of the large bowel is to absorb water and nutrients back into the blood, and to form stools which are excreted as bowel motions. The large bowel accounts for two-thirds of all colon cancer, while the rectum, which is the portion of the bowel at the very end, attached to the anus, accounts for one-third of all cases.

Risk Factors for Bowel Cancer

There are many different factors which can increase your risk of developing bowel cancer; these include:

- Age – 90 per cent of all bowel cancers are in women over 50 years of age.
- Certain gastrointestinal conditions – Crohn's disease and ulcerative colitis sufferers have an increased risk of bowel cancer.
- Diet – a low fibre, high fat diet with a high red meat intake has been shown to be associated with an increased risk of bowel cancer.

- Genetic problems – some genetic disorders, such as familial adenomatous polyposis, greatly increase your risk of bowel cancer.
- Having a first degree relative with bowel cancer – if a sibling, parent or child has bowel cancer your risk is doubled.
- Smoking
- Heavy alcohol intake
- Obesity
- Sedentary lifestyle

Signs and Symptoms of Bowel Cancer

Symptoms to watch out for with bowel cancer include:

- Bleeding from the rectum or blood in your stools
- A change in your normal bowel habit which lasts for more than six weeks, such as diarrhoea, constipation or an increased number of bowel motions per day
- Weight loss that is unexplained
- Abdominal pain
- The symptoms of anaemia – excessive tiredness or breathlessness

Diagnosis and Treatment of Bowel Cancer

Your doctor will refer you for a colonoscopy in your local hospital if it is thought that your symptoms are suggestive of bowel cancer. A colonoscopy is an inspection of your bowel using a flexible tube containing a camera. You will be given medication to drink for 24 hours prior to the test, which flushes out any faeces within the bowel, so that the best possible view can be obtained. If any suspicious areas are seen, they are biopsied to confirm the diagnosis.

If you are confirmed as having bowel cancer, it needs to be staged so that the right treatment can be offered to you. This may include surgery to remove part or all of the bowel, chemotherapy or radio-therapy. In some cases, if the cancer is in the rectum, a colostomy may be required. This is when the bowel is made to open out onto the abdominal wall, and a bag is put in place to collect any waste products. This may be temporary or permanent.

Screening for Bowel Cancer in Ireland

A national programme to start screening for bowel cancer in the 60 to 69-year-old age group was introduced in late 2012. The test checks for blood in the bowel motion by using a chemical reaction. The patient obtains a sample of their stool, completes the test at home and sends it to the laboratory for analysis via freepost. The result will be abnormal in a small percentage of cases, and these people are called for a colonoscopy. The program will eventually extend to include the 55 to 74-year-old age group.

Lung Cancer

Lung cancer is mostly seen in the 70 to 79-year-old age group. It is also associated with smoking in 85 to 90 per cent of cases. The lungs are also a common place for secondary tumours, or metasta-ses, to grow, when the original source of the cancer is elsewhere. Unfortunately, the signs and symptoms of lung cancer usually do not appear early in the disease and, as a result, the cancer can be quite advanced by the time it is diagnosed.

Signs and Symptoms of Lung Cancer

- Persistent cough or a change in a longstanding 'smoker's cough'

- Any blood coughed up at all
- Weight loss
- Shortness of breath
- Chest pain

Diagnosis and Treatment of Lung Cancer

Lung cancer is usually diagnosed by an x-ray or CT scan of the chest. Treatment options include surgery with smaller cancers which have not spread, and chemotherapy and radiotherapy if the cancer is more widespread.

Remember that your risk of lung cancer increases with the number of years you have smoked, and the number of cigarettes. If you stop smoking, you can still greatly reduce your risk of developing lung cancer.

Malignant Melanoma

Melanoma accounts for only 10 per cent of all skin cancers, but it causes the most deaths of all skin cancers. This is because it is considered to be an aggressive type of cancer; in other words, it spreads quickly, making it harder to cure. The main cause of melanoma is overexposure to the sun.

Melanomas can occur anywhere on the body, but the most common areas affected are the arms, legs, back and face. They can arise from pre-existing moles or appear for the first time.

Check that Mole

Features of a worrying mole can be checked with this list:
- **A** stands for asymmetrical – a melanoma has an irregular shape.
- **B** stands for border – a melanoma will have an irregular border or edge to it, unlike a healthy mole.

- **C** stands for colour – a melanoma will have two or more colours or shades of brown.
- **D** stands for diameter – melanomas are bigger than 6 mm (a quarter of an inch), unlike normal moles.
- **E** stands for elevated – melanomas are usually raised or elevated above normal skin.

Causes and Risk Factors of Melanoma

The main cause of melanoma is exposure to sunlight. Both ultraviolet A (UVA) and ultraviolet B (UVB), which are contained in sunlight, will damage skin over time. Use of tanning beds and sunlamps also has a similar effect.

Other risk factors for developing melanoma include:

- Having pale skin
- Having red or blonde hair
- Having blue eyes
- Having a large number of moles
- Having a family member with melanoma
- Having a large number of freckles
- Having a condition that suppresses your immune system, such as HIV
- Taking medicines that suppress your immune system (immunosuppressants)

Diagnosis and Treatment of Melanoma

Diagnosis of melanoma is done with a biopsy of the suspicious mole. The cancer is then staged to decide on the best form of treatment. Melanoma spreads though the lymphatic channels to lymph glands. These are the same glands that become swollen when you are sick with a sore throat. However, they are located everywhere in the body, and the group of glands closest to the cancer needs to be checked for cancer cells before deciding on the best treatment. Treatment may include surgery, chemotherapy or radiotherapy depending on the degree of spread if any.

Key Points

- Non-melanoma skin cancer and breast cancer are the most common cancers in Irish women.
- Cancer risk in general increases with advancing age, obesity and smoking.
- While having a family history of breast cancer or the BRCA 1 or BRCA 2 genes increases your risk of developing breast cancer, most breast cancers are not genetic, that is to say that there is no gene which specifically causes breast cancer.
- Screening for breast, colon and cervical cancer is now available in Ireland.
- Any unusual symptoms should always be reported to your doctor as soon as possible, as early detection of cancer greatly improves your chances of living a long and healthy life.

6

Infertility

Infertility is an increasingly common problem faced by couples in more recent times, with about one in seven couples experiencing a delay in conceiving. This is due to several reasons:

- Women are more commonly 'putting off' pregnancy until an older age.
- Widespread use of the combined pill masks underlying problems like irregular periods.
- Increased rate of pelvic infection, in particular chlamydia, due to an increased number of sexual partners.

When trying to conceive, regular intercourse is usually accepted to be three times a week during the week of ovulation, and twice a week in the other weeks of your cycle. Some 84 per cent of couples without fertility problems will have conceived in twelve months of regular sexual intercourse without using contraception. Therefore, couples who having been trying for twelve months or more should be investigated for possible infertility. For women aged 35 or older, investigations should be done after six months of trying to conceive.

Infertility can be divided into primary infertility, which describes women who have never been pregnant before, and secondary infertility, where the woman has had a prior pregnancy.

Causes of Infertility

Causes of infertility can be divided into several categories, as follows:

- Male infertility – this accounts for 30 per cent of cases of infertility.
- Ovulation disorders – this accounts for 25 per cent of cases of infertility.
- Unexplained infertility – this accounts for 20 per cent of cases of infertility.
- Problems with the uterus (womb) and fallopian tubes, as well as various other causes, account for 25 per cent of cases of infertility.

Male Infertility

Semen is the liquid produced within a man's reproductive system, which contains sperm. There are several problems which can occur with sperm, including the following:

- The number of sperm can be reduced.
- The movement (motility) of the sperm can be reduced.
- The shape (morphology) of the sperm can be abnormal.

In a lot of cases the cause of abnormal semen is not found, but there are several known factors which can affect the quality and quantity of sperm contained in semen, as follows:

- Testicles are the manufacturing and storage centre for sperm. If they are damaged in any way this can affect sperm. Causes of damage include cancer, trauma, infection, undescended testes and surgery.

- If no sperm at all are present in the semen, this suggests a blockage, whereby sperm are being obstructed from being released into the semen, possibly due to surgery or infection.
- If a man has undergone sterilisation or vasectomy, sperm production continues but the tube which transports sperm out of the testicles has been blocked.
- Ejaculatory problems, such as premature ejaculation (ejaculation happens too quickly) or retrograde ejaculation (ejaculation occurs backwards into the bladder), can affect the quantity of sperm.
- Very low levels of male hormone, also known as hypogonadism, will prevent sperm production. This is seen with some cancers, and can be caused by the use of illegal drugs.
- Medicines and drug use, such as the drug sulphasalazine which is used in rheumatoid arthritis and Crohn's disease, chemotherapy, and anabolic steroids used illegally in body building, may affect sperm.
- Alcohol in quantities greater than 5 units per day has been shown to have an adverse affect on sperm.

Ovulation Disorders

The most common causes of ovulation disorders are polycystic ovarian syndrome (PCOS) and premature ovarian insufficiency (POI).

PCOS is a common hormone disorder seen in 5 to 10 per cent of women aged between 20 and 40. It is more commonly seen in women who are obese, but up to 20 per cent of sufferers will have a normal BMI. It is characterised by infrequent or absent ovulation, caused by abnormally high levels of androgens or male hormones in the blood.

POI is defined as the inability of the ovary to produce enough hormones to bring about regular ovulation in women under the age of 40. This is different to premature menopause, as women with POI can produce hormones from the ovaries on and off for several years and, indeed, can conceive.

Unexplained Infertility

In 20 per cent of cases of infertility no cause is found. However, it is more likely to be a problem in women over 35, so one possible theory is that it is related to the quality of the eggs being released, as we know that this declines with age. Another possible cause is mild endometriosis, a benign disease of the pelvis, where endometrium (womb lining) is found on areas outside the womb, most commonly on the ovaries.

Female Reproductive System

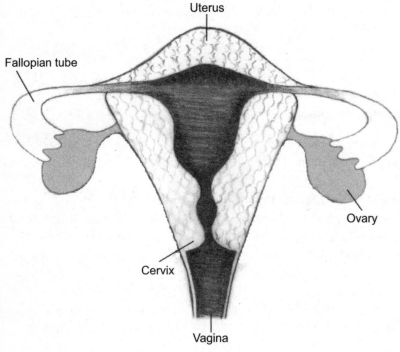

Problems with the Uterus (Womb) and Fallopian Tubes

Both the uterus and the fallopian tubes need to be healthy in order for natural conception and implantation to occur. Sperm travel down the tubes, meet the egg and fertilisation takes place. The fertilised egg then travels down to the uterus, and implantation occurs, which allows the egg to grow further. Some common problems related to the fallopian tubes and uterus include:

- Pelvic inflammatory disease (PID) – this is primarily caused by chlamydia infection, which has no symptoms in up to 80 per cent of women affected. It can cause damage to the lining of the tubes, preventing normal movement of sperm and eggs, and also cause complete blockage of one or both tubes.
- Endometriosis can cause scarring, and cysts can form, distorting the usual arrangement of the tubes and ovaries in the pelvis.
- Fibroids are benign growths of the uterus seen in up to 50 per cent of women. When they grow into the cavity of the uterus they can cause problems with blockage of the fallopian tubes or prevention of implantation.
- Pelvic surgery for any reason, notably a previous appendectomy, can cause scarring and, therefore, may disrupt the fallopian tubes.

General Factors Affecting Fertility

In more general terms, other factors affecting a couple's fertility include:

- A woman's age – after the age of 35 a woman's fertility starts to decrease more rapidly than before.
- Smoking has been shown to have a detrimental effect on both male and female fertility.

- Being overweight or underweight – an abnormal BMI adversely affects fertility for both men and women. Many fertility clinics will not proceed with treatments such as in vitro fertilisation (IVF) if your BMI is over 30.
- Stress – this can reduce your sex drive, as well as having an adverse effect on ovulation and sperm production.
- Sexually transmitted infections, in particular chlamydia, can cause fertility problems for both sexes, such as tubal damage in women and epididymo-orchitis (infection of the testes) in men.
- Occupational/environmental factors – exposure to certain chemicals, such as pesticides and some solvents, can cause fertility problems.

How to Investigate Infertility

History of the Female Partner

This can sometimes give your doctor a clue as to what might be the underlying cause of infertility, if there is one to be found. The information your doctor will ask you for should include:

- Your age
- How long you have been trying to conceive for
- The length of your cycle
- If you are aware of when you ovulate
- Your pattern of sexual intercourse, both around ovulation and during the rest of your cycle
- Whether you experience any cycle-related problems, such as pain after sex, painful periods, bleeding between periods and heavy periods
- Whether you have excessive hairiness or acne
- If you have experienced a milky discharge from your nipples
- Details of any current illnesses
- Details of any previous medical illnesses or surgeries

- Details of any previous pregnancies and their outcomes
- Your recent smear history
- Your smoking, alcohol and caffeine intake
- Details of any medications being taken or any other drug-taking
- Your diet, including any recent weight loss or gain

History of the Male Partner

Your male partner should also be asked for the following information:

- Whether he has experienced any sexual difficulty, for example with erections or ejaculation
- If he had any testicle problems as a child, such as undescended testes
- If he has a history of previous infection, in particular chlamydia or mumps
- His job description – any exposure to heat or chemicals
- Whether he has any current illnesses
- If he is taking any medications or using any drugs, in particular anabolic steroids or marijuana
- His smoking, caffeine and alcohol intake
- Whether he has fathered a child in the past

Physical Examination

Examination of the Female Partner

For the woman, physical examination is mostly done to look for signs of a hormonal imbalance called polycystic ovarian syndrome (PCOS). So your doctor may be looking for a high BMI, excessive hairiness (especially on the face) and acne. Pelvic examination may show an area of tenderness in the pelvis, which might indicate the presence of infection or endometriosis.

Examination of the Male Partner

For the man, the examination involves assessing the size of the testicles and also to check for a varicocele. A varicocele is a dilated vein in the scrotum, which has a distinctive feel on examination – often described as a 'bag of worms'. It can cause some problems with sperm quality, and is easily treated with surgery.

Tests Which Should be Done

Tests on the Female Partner

- Blood tests should be performed at two different times during a menstrual cycle:
  - Between day 2 and 4, the following tests are done: follicle-stimulating hormone (FSH); luteinising hormone (LH); rubella status; prolactin; and thyroid-stimulating Hormone (TSH). If there is an irregular cycle, then testosterone, sex hormone binding globulin (SHBG), androstenedione and 17-hydroxyprogesterone tests should also be done.
  - A progesterone level should be taken seven days before your next period. This is sometimes called the day 21 proges-terone test, as the typical cycle is 28 days long. However, many women will have longer or shorter cycles.
  - The level of anti-Müllerian hormone (AMH) found in the blood is an accurate measure of ovarian reserve, i.e. the number of unripened follicles remaining in the ovaries. This test should be done if premature ovarian insufficiency is suspected and in all women who need fertility proce-dures, as it is an accurate predictor of their success. It can be done on any day of the menstrual cycle.
- A pelvic ultrasound is done in the first half of the menstrual cycle. This is to demonstrate any abnormalities in the uterus.

- A test to check the fallopian tubes can also be done. This can either be done by:
  - Performing a laparoscopy, which is a surgical procedure performed under full anaesthetic, whereby a camera is inserted into the pelvis to directly examine the pelvic organs
  - An x-ray called a hysterosalpingogram (HSG), which involves pushing dye up through the cervix and observing the dye filling the tubes and then spilling out of both ends of the tubes, to confirm that the tubes are open

Tests on the Male Partner

Semen analysis is a detailed examination of the semen to check for many different features, such as the number and shape of sperm, and their ability to move efficiently. Normally, the male partner is asked to abstain from sex for a few days before collecting his sample for analysis to allow the sample to be as good as possible, and it is often repeated if the first result is abnormal, as this does not always mean that there is a significant problem.

Infertility Treatments

The most suitable treatment option for you and your partner will depend on lots of different factors, including the cause of your delay in conceiving if one is identified, and your age. Treatment options also vary depending on where you pursue your infertility treatment, but I have outlined below some of the more common treatments and the infertility causes for which they are used.

Clomiphene Citrate (Clomid)

This is the most common medication used for ovulation induction, i.e. encouraging the release of a ripened egg during a cycle.

Clomiphene works as an anti-oestrogen in the brain. This tricks the body into thinking that there is no oestrogen and, accordingly, the pituitary and ovaries produce lots of extra hormone, causing an exaggerated response from the ovaries. It is used in PCOS and other non-ovulating conditions. It is also used by couples who have unexplained infertility, and this is known as 'super ovulation'.

Clomiphene is a tablet given for five consecutive days, usually days 3–7 of a menstrual cycle. Clomiphene will achieve ovulation in about 75 per cent of women, but it is unlikely to achieve pregnancy after six cycles. The normal recommendation is to use it for no longer than three to six months. Follicle tracking is recommended when using clomiphene. This is the use of ovarian ultrasound during the cycle, usually around day 11 to day 13. This demonstrates whether the medication is achieving the level of ovarian stimulation needed to produce an egg, and also to give you an idea of when to have sex to coincide with ovulation. The size of the developing follicles is measured, and when one follicle reaches 16 mm to 17 mm, then ovulation is expected to occur in the next 24 hours, and timed intercourse is advised. If sufficient follicle development is not seen, the clomiphene dose can be increased. Conversely, if the degree of stimulation seen in the ovaries is thought to be too much, the couple are advised not to have sex for the rest of that cycle to avoid conception on that particular cycle.

Side effects are usually very mild and include hot flushes, abdominal bloating and mood swings. Multiple pregnancy is also a side effect, and occurs in approximately 8 per cent of all clomiphene pregnancies.

Metformin (Glucophage)

This is a medication traditionally used in the management of diabetes. It can be used as an ovulation induction agent on its own, but it is most useful when used with clomiphene for women who have proven resistant to clomiphene alone, i.e. no ovulation has occurred when using clomiphene in isolation.

Gonadotrophins

These are medications which are similar to the hormone signals from the brain that stimulate the ovaries. They are given by injection, either by the patient herself or her partner, on a daily basis from early in the cycle up until ovulation. Common gonadotrophin preparations used are Puregon, Menopur and Gonal F. Ultrasound is required at the beginning of a treatment cycle, and then again a few days later.

Human Chorionic Gonadotrophin (hCG)

This is a hormone which is given as an injection and is used to trigger ovulation. It is administered only when one or two follicles less than 17 mm in diameter are seen. If more than three follicles are seen, the cycle is cancelled. It is used when clomiphene is being used with intrauterine insemination, and in all FSH-stimulated cycles. It is also given three and five days after ovulation to improve success rates.

Ovarian Hyperstimulation Syndrome (OHSS)

This is a potentially serious complication of all ovulation induction and super ovulation fertility cycles. It is not well understood, but FSH and clomiphene can cause an excessive reaction by the ovaries. Large amounts of oestrogen are produced, and you can experience swelling of the abdomen, pain and nausea. Pregnancy makes this condition much worse; hence, if overstimulation is suspected on ultrasound, the couple will be advised to avoid conception for that cycle, and the OHSS usually resolves over time.

Intrauterine Insemination (IUI)

This is a procedure which involves collecting a sperm sample from your partner, and placing it into the womb or uterus at the time of ovulation. This is usually combined with ovarian-stimulating drugs, such as clomiphene or FSH injections.

The sperm sample is prepared in such a way as to only use the best quality sperm. These are then placed directly into the womb using a tiny tube. This is not painful and is done as an outpatient procedure. IUI is used for couples with mild sperm abnormalities, some cases of unexplained infertility, and some conditions where there are sexual problems, such as erection problems, or when vaginal penetration is not possible due to pain (vaginismus).

IUI is not usually recommended if the female partner is over 38 years of age, if there are significant sperm abnormalities or if significant endometriosis is present.

Laparoscopy

Laparoscopy, as described earlier, is a procedure done under general anaesthetic which is used to diagnose female fertility problems, but also to treat certain conditions to maximise your fertility. It can be used to reduce endometriosis by burning off spots of the disease, as well as breaking down scar tissue which may have developed. It can also be used to perform a procedure called ovarian drilling. This is used in women who have PCOS which is proving resistant to FSH stimulation. Several small holes are 'drilled' into the surface of the ovary during the laparoscopy, which can improve stimulation or even natural ovulation for a few cycles after the procedure.

Tubal Surgery

This is not commonly done, but if tubal damage is not very extensive, then surgery can be an option. More often, IVF is offered as the best option if the fallopian tubes are badly affected by previous infection or endometriosis. It is also used for reversal of female sterilisation, where the fallopian tubes have been deliberately blocked in the past for permanent contraception.

Artificial Reproductive Technology (ART)

This is the term used to describe all the technologies available to us that involve fertilisation outside the woman's body, followed by transfer back into the womb and subsequent implantation.

These include:

- In vitro fertilisation (IVF)
- Intracytoplasmic sperm injection (ICSI)
- Frozen embryo transfer (FET)
- Blastocyst transfer

In Vitro Fertilisation (IVF)

IVF is the best known of all ARTs. It has been used to help women conceive since 1978 and can be very successful, depending on the reason it is required. Common reasons why IVF is used include:

- Blocked fallopian tubes
- Some cases of male factor infertility
- Multiple failed fertility treatments
- Use of donated eggs or embryos

After lengthy counselling, an IVF cycle usually begins by suppressing the woman's hormones using a nasal spray. Daily injections are then started, during which time the ovaries are being stimulated and, therefore, followed closely by scan. A hCG injection is given when the follicles have reached the appropriate size, and 36 hours later the eggs are collected. This is a simple and mostly painless procedure. The eggs are then combined with sperm collected from the male partner, and the eggs and sperm are incubated together for two to three days until they have fertilised and started to increase in size. These are now called embryos, and one or two are put back into the womb. Pregnancy tests are done fourteen days later.

Intracytoplasmic Sperm Injection (ICSI)

This is similar to IVF but is used more commonly when there are few healthy sperm available. Instead of combining several hundred thousand sperm with one egg to allow spontaneous fertilisation to take place, one healthy sperm is injected directly into the egg to allow fertilisation to happen. The embryo is then put back into the womb, as with IVF.

Frozen Embryo Transfer (FET)

Often during an IVF cycle, if there has been a good ovarian response with lots of eggs retrieved, there will be a surplus of embryos. Only one or two embryos are replaced, so the remaining embryos are frozen and stored in the fertility clinic for future use. These can be defrosted and used when needed by the couple. About 70 per cent of frozen embryos will survive the defrosting process, and then can be replaced to achieve pregnancy.

Blastocyst Transfer

This is a newer technology which is becoming more popular in fertility clinics. A blastocyst is the name given to the fertilised egg about four to five days after fertilisation. It is now a small ball of cells. By delaying the transfer back into the womb some studies suggest that the success rates are higher. Only one blastocyst is transferred.

Key Points

- Infertility affects one in seven couples, and this figure is rising.
- Couples trying to conceive for twelve months or longer should seek help.
- Where the female partner is aged 35 or older, the couple should seek help after six months.
- Male factor infertility accounts for 30 per cent of all cases of infertility.
- Basic investigations include blood tests on day 3 and day 21, a pelvic ultrasound and semen analysis.

7

Sexually Transmitted Infections

Sexually transmitted infections (STIs) are those infections which are spread from one person to another through some form of sexual contact. More sexually-liberated times, and a more relaxed attitude towards sexuality, have brought about some significant changes in the sexual behaviour of Irish women. These changes are both positive and negative.

One of the more undesirable changes includes an alarming increase in the incidence of STIs. There are several reasons why this may have come about: women are having more sexual partners at all stages in their lives, and contraception has also improved in recent years. The effectiveness of hormone-containing contraception has helped to prevent pregnancy, which has led to less condom usage and a resultant increase in STIs.

On the other hand, a positive change includes a more frank and open approach to sex and STIs, with women more likely to confide in their doctor about their worries. There is a common misconception that vaginal penetration is the only way of transmitting one of these infections. In fact all forms of sexual contact, including skin-to-skin genital contact, kissing, and anal and oral sex, are also methods of easily transmitting some infections.

This chapter covers the main STIs which are both seen by doctors and are the main sources of worry for sexually active women.

Chlamydia

Chlamydia is a common STI caused by a bacterium called *Chlamydia trachomatis*. It is most commonly transmitted through anal or vaginal sex, although it can be transmitted through oral sex. It can also infect the eyes. It is known as a silent disease because up to 75 per cent of infected women have no symptoms. However, it can be detected 72 hours after exposure by a simple test. If symptoms do occur, they usually appear within one to three weeks after sexual contact with an infected person. If untreated, chlamydia infection can lead to chronic pelvic pain, infertility and ectopic pregnancy.

Symptoms and Treatment of Chlamydia

Symptoms include an abnormal vaginal discharge or a burning sensation when urinating. If pelvic infection follows, you may experience lower abdominal pain, nausea, fever, pain during intercourse or bleeding between periods. Chlamydia infection is diagnosed either by taking a swab from the cervix or by urine sample. It is easily treated and cured with antibiotics. All sexual partners should be tested and treated. You and your partner should then abstain from sexual contact for a further three weeks after completing your treatment. It is important if you have been diagnosed with chlamydia that any of your recent sexual partners be notified of your diagnosis to try to contain the spread of the infection.

Human Papillomavirus (Which Causes Genital Warts)

This is a very common virus which is transmitted through genital skin contact. It is estimated that 80 per cent of sexually active women are infected with genital human papillomavirus (HPV) infection at some point in their lives.

Signs and Symptoms of HPV

The majority of women infected have no idea that they are infected with the virus. HPV lives in the genital skin and usually causes no symptoms. Most women will clear the infection on their own over a period of three to five years. Some women get visible genital warts, or have pre-cancerous changes in the cervix.

Genital warts normally appear as soft, flesh-coloured lumps, usually in the genital area. They can be raised or flat, single or multiple, small or large. They can appear on the vulva, in or around the vagina or anus, or on the cervix. After sexual contact with an infected person, warts may appear within weeks or months, or not at all.

Diagnosis and Treatment of Genital Warts

Genital warts are diagnosed by inspecting the area, usually by a doctor. Visible warts can be removed by medication applied by the patient, or by treatments performed by their doctor using liquid nitrogen, very similar to the usual treatment for warts on hands and feet. This is called cryotherapy.

Is There a Cure for HPV?

Unfortunately, there is no cure for HPV infection. The treatments available are designed to treat the symptoms caused by the virus, such as warts and pre-cancerous changes in the cervix. For those women whose HPV infection persists, regular smear tests are essential to ensure that the pre-cancerous changes caused by HPV do not progress to cervical cancer (see Chapter 5).

Gonorrhoea

Gonorrhoea is another STI which causes little or no symptoms in women. It is caused by a bacterium called *Neisseria gonorrhoeae*, which can be transmitted through all forms of sexual contact. The symptoms can be vague and easily confused with a bladder or vaginal infection. The initial signs and symptoms include pain when urinating, increased vaginal discharge and vaginal bleeding between periods. It is diagnosed by a swab test from the cervix or water passage (urethra), and is easily treated with antibiotics. Gonorrhoea is a common cause of pelvic inflammatory disease (PID). This can lead to infertility, chronic pain and ectopic pregnancy.

Trichomonas

This is a sexually transmitted disease caused by a parasite called *Trichomonas vaginalis*. It usually causes an unpleasant, foul-smelling, yellow-green discharge from the vagina. It can also cause vaginal itching or discomfort during sex. However, nearly 50 per cent of cases are detected during routine STI screening because you may have no symptoms. This infection is usually treated with an anti-biotic taken orally called metronidazole (Flagyl). Male partners should also be treated with similar medication.

Pubic Lice or Crabs

This is an infection caused by a parasite called *Phthirus pubis*. These are lice which are passed from one person to another through genital contact. They live mostly in coarse hair, such as pubic hair, but occa-sionally they can be found in other hairy areas, although the scalp is rarely affected. Symptoms include an onset of itchiness in the pubic area within 7 to 21 days of sexual contact with an infected person. The lice are visible to the naked eye. Treatment involves using an insecticide cream or lotion on the pubic area and leaving it on for 12 to 24 hours. This needs to be repeated seven days later. Bed linen and towels used while infected should be washed at a high temperature, and sexual contacts within the last month should be contacted.

Genital Herpes

This is an STI caused by the herpes simplex virus (HSV).The first outbreak usually occurs within two weeks of contact with an infected person. Most women have no symptoms or signs from this infection. When signs do occur, they appear as one or more painful blisters around the genital area. These blisters break down, leaving tender sores that may take between two and four weeks to heal.

Symptoms, Diagnosis and Treatment

Apart from genital pain, you can experience flu-like symptoms and swollen glands. Genital herpes is diagnosed by visual inspection and swabbing of the sores. If it is the first known attack of genital herpes, the symptoms will be greatly improved by taking medication prescribed by a doctor, and this will shorten the duration of symptoms. Typically another outbreak can appear weeks or months after the first, but it is almost always less severe and shorter than the first. This is called a recurrence. With recurrences, there is only a benefit in starting medication as soon as symptoms appear. Recurrences often start as a tingling sensation on genital skin, and if this happens, then a course of tablets will help to prevent a full-blown recurrence. Most sufferers can expect four to five recurrences in the first year. Although the infection can stay in the body indefinitely, the number of recurrences usually decreases over a period of years.

Spread of Genital Herpes

The virus is released from the sores, but it can also be released between outbreaks from skin that does not appear to be broken or to have a sore. The virus can spread from an infected partner who does not have a visible sore and may not know he or she is infected. There are two types of herpes simplex – HSV-1 and HSV-2. Previously

HSV-2 was the most common type of genital herpes found, and it is only spread through genital contact. It tends to cause more recurrences and causes more severe symptoms. However, in more recent times, due to changing sexual behaviour patterns, HSV-1 has become a more common cause of genital herpes. HSV-1 is probably better known as the cause of blisters on the lips known as cold sores. HSV-1 infection of the genitals is usually caused by contact with a person who has HSV-1 infection on their lips.

HIV

Human immunodeficiency virus (HIV) is a virus that causes acquired immunodeficiency syndrome or AIDS. AIDS is a condition in which the immune system begins to fail, leading to life-threatening infections. Infection with HIV occurs by the transfer of blood, semen, vaginal fluid, pre-ejaculate or breast milk. The four major routes of transmission are unsafe sex, dirty needles, consumption of breast milk and transmission from an infected mother to her baby at birth (vertical transmission). Medication reduces both the number of people who die from the disease and the seriousness of infections that the HIV-positive person gets.

Most people infected with HIV eventually develop AIDS. They mostly die from infections or cancers as a result of their immune system slowly breaking down. HIV progresses to AIDS differently for everyone, but taking anti-HIV medication will dramatically slow this down. Treatment with anti-retroviral medication increases the life expectancy of people infected with HIV. With modern medication, being HIV positive is now considered to be similar to having a chronic disease, such as diabetes, which requires lifelong treatment, but should not greatly shorten the life expectancy of the infected person. Even after HIV has progressed to AIDS, the average survival time with medication is estimated to be more than five years. Without medication, someone who has AIDS typically dies within a year.

HIV Testing

There are a steady number of newly-diagnosed cases of HIV every year in Ireland. It is also known that there are a significant number of undiagnosed HIV-positive men and women who pose a real threat due to their lack of awareness of their HIV status. There have been recent calls for more HIV testing to be done during routine visits to the doctor. It is very important to have regular testing if you are sexually active, to protect yourself and your sexual partners. HIV is detected by a simple blood test, but this should be repeated three months after possible exposure, as there may be a delay in showing a HIV-positive result.

Hepatitis B

Hepatitis B is a virus which causes liver disease. Ways of becoming infected with hepatitis B include being born to a mother with hepatitis B, having sex with an infected person, being tattooed or pierced with unsterilised tools that were used on an infected person, getting an accidental needle stick with a needle that was used on an infected person, using an infected person's razor or toothbrush, or sharing drug needles with an infected person.

Signs and Symptoms of Hepatitis B

Hepatitis B usually has no symptoms. Children, especially infants, are more likely to get chronic hepatitis B, which usually has no symptoms until signs of liver damage appear. Your immune system can clear hepatitis B from the body, but some of those affected will go on to develop chronic hepatitis, children in particular. Without treatment, chronic hepatitis B can cause scarring of the liver (called cirrhosis), liver cancer and liver failure.

Diagnosis and Treatment of Hepatitis B

Hepatitis B is diagnosed through blood tests, which should be done immediately after possible infection and again after three months. This is because there may be a delay in the blood test showing positive for hepatitis B. The infection is not usually treated unless it becomes chronic, when it is treated with drugs that slow or stop the virus from damaging the liver.

Hepatitis C

Hepatitis C, like hepatitis B, is a liver disease caused by a virus. The ways you can become infected with hepatitis C are identical to hepatitis B (see above). Most people have no symptoms until the virus causes liver damage, which can take ten or more years to happen. It can be easily tested by your doctor with a blood test. This should be done immediately after possible infection, and then repeated after three months, as there can be a delay in the virus showing up in blood tests.

Most hepatitis C infections become chronic. This means that the virus cannot be cleared by the immune system and stays in the body indefinitely. Without treatment, chronic hepatitis C can cause cirrhosis, liver cancer and liver failure. Like hepatitis B, it is only treated if it becomes chronic.

Syphilis

Syphilis is caused by the bacterium *Treponema pallidum*. It is a disease that is rarely seen nowadays, but there are outbreaks that occur sporadically, particularly amongst sex workers. Syphilis is passed from person to person through direct contact with a syphilis sore. Sores occur mainly on the external genitals, vagina or anus, or in the rectum. Sores can also occur on the lips and in the mouth. Transmission of the infection happens during vaginal, anal or oral sex. Pregnant women with the disease can pass it to the babies they are carrying. Many people infected with syphilis do not have any symptoms for years, yet remain at risk for late-stage complications if they are not treated.

Stages of Syphilis

The primary stage of syphilis is characterised by the appearance of a single sore. The time between infection with syphilis and the start of the first symptom can range from 10 to 90 days (average 21 days). It appears at the spot where syphilis entered the body. The sore lasts for between three and six weeks, and it heals without treatment. However, if adequate treatment is not administered, the infection progresses.

Skin rashes typically characterise the next stage. This stage usually starts with the development of a rash on one or more areas of the body. In addition to rashes, symptoms may include fever, swollen lymph glands or a sore throat.

The late stages of syphilis can develop in about 15 per cent of people who have not been treated for syphilis, and can appear ten to twenty years after infection was first acquired. This late stage can cause problems with coordinating muscle movements, paralysis, numbness, gradual blindness and dementia.

Diagnosis and Treatment of Syphilis

The diagnosis can be made either with a swab from the genital ulcer or by blood test, as shortly after infection occurs the body produces syphilis antibodies. A low level of antibodies will likely stay in the blood for months or years even after the disease has been successfully treated.

Genital sores caused by syphilis make it easier to transmit and acquire HIV infection sexually. There is an estimated two to five times increased risk of acquiring HIV if exposed to it when syphilis is present.

Syphilis is easy to cure in its early stages. A single injection of penicillin – an antibiotic – will cure a person who has had syphilis for less than a year, but there is no cure for late-stage syphilis.

Protect Yourself from STIs

Unfortunately, the number of cases of STIs has continued to rise steeply in recent years. That means that your risk of getting an STI from a sexual partner is higher now than ever before. Abstinence is the only guaranteed way of protecting yourself, but if that isn't possible the next best thing is to always use a condom, although this doesn't protect you completely. A new development in recent years is for you and your new partner to both have STI screening before becoming sexually intimate. This allows you to start a new sexual relationship with a clean slate. And don't forget – if you are diagnosed with an STI, have a full screening for all other STIs. Up to 20 per cent of women who are diagnosed with one STI will have another at the same time.

Key Points

- The numbers of women getting STIs is increasing in Ireland.
- Genital warts and chlamydia are the most common STIs seen.
- Treatments for STIs are usually quick and effective.
- With viruses such as HIV and hepatitis it is vital to detect them in the early stages to control the disease.

8

Contraception

Contraception has been around for thousands of years, providing women with the freedom to control their fertility with varying degrees of success. In more modern times breakthroughs in technology have allowed for new, more advanced forms of contraception, which have provided a greater choice for the modern woman. There is still a long way to go in the development of the 'perfect contraceptive', but below I explain the main types available to women at the moment.

Effectiveness of Contraceptives

Method	Percentage of Women with Pregnancy After 1 Year of Use	
	Lowest Expected	Typical
No method	85.00	85.00
Oestrogen/progestogen combination pill	0.10	3.00
Progestogen only pill	0.50	3.00
IUS Mirena coil	0.10	0.10
IUD copper coil	0.60	0.80
Implant	0.10	0.10

(Continued)

(Continued)

Method	Percentage of Women with Pregnancy After 1 Year of Use	
	Lowest Expected	Typical
Depo-Provera	0.30	0.30
Female sterilisation	0.40	0.40
Male sterilisation	0.15	0.10
Withdrawal	4.00	19.00
Spermicides	6.00	18.00
Male condoms	3.00	12.00
Female condoms	5.00	21.00
Calendar method	9.00	20.50
Basal body temperature method	2.00	20.50

Source: adapted from Trussell, J., 2004, 'The Essentials of Contraception: Efficacy, Safety, and Personal Considerations', in R.A. Hatcher *et al* (editors), *Contraceptive Technology*, 18th edition, New York: Ardent Media, pp. 221–252.

Natural Methods

For some women a form of pregnancy prevention is needed, but a natural form which does not involve either hormones or devices is preferable. There are many different types which can be used, but they all have one thing in common: all the methods are based on prediction of ovulation and, therefore, your most fertile time of the month. The failure rate is higher than with other forms of contraception (see figure). This is because there can be variation in your menstrual cycle from month to month, and external factors can influence the signs of ovulation that are being closely observed. Natural methods of contraception also depend on a level of self-control from you and your partner, for varying lengths of time during each cycle.

The basis of all natural forms of contraception is that you abstain or not be sexually active during that portion of your menstrual cycle when you are fertile. These methods are also called fertility awareness methods and are also used when trying to conceive. The methods heighten your awareness of the menstrual cycle and the most fertile part of the cycle in which to try to conceive.

The various methods involve trying to predict the portion of your cycle during which you should abstain from sex. This portion of the menstrual cycle comprises the days before ovulation or egg release from the ovaries, the day of ovulation itself, and for several days after that.

Because an egg can survive for up to 24 hours after ovulation and sperm can survive for up to 72 hours or longer, the period of abstinence can be a substantial portion of the cycle. Natural methods of contraception can be up to 98 per cent effective, but to achieve this level of success self-control and significant levels of monitoring are required.

Calendar Rhythm Method

This is based on information from twelve previous menstrual cycles. Eighteen days are subtracted from the shortest cycle noted, and this denotes the first possible fertile day. Eleven days are subtracted from the longest cycle noted, and this marks the last possible fertile day on the calendar. Obviously, if your menstrual cycle is irregular, then the period of abstinence will be significantly longer.

Basal Body Temperature Method

This method is based on the fact that your body temperature drops slightly between 12 and 24 hours before ovulation occurs, and then rises again once an egg has been released. This drop in temperature is very small – approximately half a degree centigrade. The method involves taking your temperature every morning before getting out of bed, using a special thermometer which detects small changes in temperature. You should abstain from sex from the time of your period until the drop in temperature is noted, and you should continue to abstain from sex until the temperature rises again and for a further 72 hours thereafter.

Mucus Inspection Method

This method is based on the changes in your cervical mucus at different times in your menstrual cycle. When oestrogen levels rise approaching ovulation, cervical mucus changes to a thin stretchy consistency, which can be stretched between two fingers up to 1 inch. Some experience is required to interpret cervical mucus, and for this method, as for all the other natural methods, it is recommended that a few 'practice' cycles be completed without relying on it for contraception until you are comfortable that you can spot these subtle changes. Mucus observation can be on underpants, toilet paper or by gently collecting mucus from the vaginal opening with two fingers. Sex should be avoided from when the mucus is first noted to change and for a further four days.

Barrier Contraception

Barrier contraceptive methods include the male condom, female condom and diaphragm. These act as a barrier to sperm in order to prevent fertilisation. They are cheap, contain no hormones, provide significant protection against STIs (condoms only) and are used during sex only, removing the need for continuous use of any contraception. However, the failure rates with barrier contraceptives are higher than other forms of contraception, mostly due to a poor knowledge of how to use them correctly.

Male Condoms

These are also known as sheaths or prophylactics. They are mostly made of latex, but for latex allergy sufferers a polyurethane condom is available. The condom is placed on the erect penis prior to penetration, taking care to leave a half inch of empty condom at the tip to allow for semen collection. After ejaculation, the penis should be withdrawn slowly while holding firmly on to the condom to avoid any spillage of semen. Other than abstinence, condoms are the best protection against STIs.

Female Condom

This is a polyurethane tube, closed at one end, with a ring at each end. It is inserted into the vagina by the woman up to 8 hours before sex. It is removed after sex and discarded. This is much less well-known than the male condom, and the reasons for its lack of popularity as a form of contraception are many. Firstly, it is awkward to use and can be difficult to insert. Allergic reactions to the polyurethane can be a problem. It also has a higher failure rate than male condoms.

Diaphragm

This is a soft, flexible, dome-shaped device which is made of rubber. The diaphragm offers a reasonably reliable form of contraception which can be used 'on demand', rather than having to use something continuously. They are made in different sizes and, initially, a doctor fits you with the right size diaphragm. You are then taught how to insert and remove it by the doctor until you are confident using it. It is inserted by you no more than 4 hours before sex and must be used with spermicide at the same time. It creates a barrier at the top of the vagina, preventing the passage of sperm through the cervix. The diaphragm should be left in the vagina for 6 to 8 hours after sex, and then removed.

Diaphragms last up to two years, but if there has been any significant weight loss, or if you have had a pregnancy, then you should be re-assessed as you may need a change in diaphragm size. Urinary tract infections can occur as a side effect of diaphragm use.

Hormonal Contraception

There are two hormones used in hormonal contraception, both of which are artificially manufactured to try and copy the hormones that ovaries produce in women. Those hormones are oestrogen and progesterone. Their effects on the body are slightly different, and their methods of preventing pregnancy also differ, as do their failure rates. They are used in two main forms:

- Oestrogen/progesterone combinations – also known as 'the pill'
- Progesterone only

Oestrogen/Progesterone Combinations

This hormonal form of contraception is a combination of oestrogen – either a synthetic alternative, called ethinylestradiol, or 17β oestradiol – with a synthetic form of progesterone, called a progestogen. These progestogens can be norethisterone, dydrogesterone, drospirenone or gestodene. These two hormones suppress the actions of the ovaries, which in turn feeds back to the brain, and the hormonal signalling system to the ovaries is temporarily shut down. The hormonal combination delivers a balanced dose of hormone every day for 21 to 24 days, followed by a period of withdrawal from the pill, during which time the lining of the womb or endometrium bleeds. The withdrawal period from the pill is four to seven days. The combined pill's mechanism of action is prevention of ovulation, and it has a very low failure rate when taken properly.

Taking the Pill

Most women can safely use the combined pill as contraception. However, if you have high blood pressure (hypertension), a history of blood clots or a family history of blood clots, if you are obese, or if you have a history of certain types of severe migraine, you are probably not suitable for the combined pill. If you smoke over the age of 35 the combined pill cannot be offered to you as a form of contraception.

Your doctor will normally recommend that you start your first packet of pills during a period. This is to ensure that you are not pregnant when starting. If you start on day 1, then your contraceptive cover starts from that first day onwards. Otherwise, if you start it on any other day, you cannot rely on it as contraception until you have taken seven pills in a row. If you are going to start the pill at some point during your cycle other than during your period, it is a good idea to check with your doctor first. It is a completely safe thing to do, but you may experience some unwanted side effects, such as bleeding, in the initial stages. Depending on the brand used, 21 to 24 pills are taken consecutively. This is followed by a pill-free break of four to seven days, during which a bleed occurs, which is referred to as a withdrawal bleed. This is much lighter and shorter than your usual period. After the pill-free interval is over a new pack is started.

Other Methods of Combined Contraception

There are several different ways of using combined contraception. The most widely used is that of a pill taken orally. However, in recent years, other ways of taking hormonal combined contraception have been developed. One increasingly popular way is that of the vaginal ring. This is a soft plastic ring which is coated with the required hormones. You can easily insert it into the vagina yourself and it is left there for 21 days. During this time a continuous release of hormone occurs from the ring which prevents ovulation. It is removed for seven days and a withdrawal bleed occurs. The advantages of the ring are that you can avoid having to remember to take a daily pill, and the hormone dose is lower than the tablet version.

Contraceptive Patches are also available, which release the hormone dose into the bloodstream through the skin via weekly patches that you apply, with a seven-day withdrawal period monthly. Skin irritation can be a problem with patches. Pregnancy rates are as low with these non-oral types of contraception as with the tablet forms.

Benefits of Combined Contraception

Apart from contraception, there are other benefits from using combined contraception. If you are experiencing very heavy periods, or menorrhagia, you can use the pill to control this with great effect. Although for contraceptive purposes the lowest possible dose of oestrogen is always better, this is not always the case with period control. Sometimes, a slightly increased dose of oestrogen is required to do this efficiently. The same is true for painful periods, or dysmenorrhoea. This can be dramatically reduced using combined contraception, but a higher dose may be needed.

The incidence of pelvic inflammatory disease (PID), which is usually caused by chlamydia, is also reduced with pill usage, as is the incidence of benign or non-cancerous breast disease, such as cysts.

Premenstrual syndrome (PMS) can also be greatly improved using combined contraception. PMS is a collection of symptoms experienced by a lot of women in the days coming up to a period. They include mood swings, irritability, tiredness and breast tenderness.

Acne in women, either due to a hormonal imbalance or not, can be significantly improved with combined contraception.

Although combined contraception is designed to allow a withdrawal bleed monthly, this does not have to be the case. Often with severe dysmenorrhoea the woman is advised to use the pill 'back to back', i.e. to follow on immediately from the end of one pack of pills to a new pack. This avoids the pill-free interval of seven days and, therefore, the bleed. This can be safely done for several months in a row. There are no long-term adverse effects associated with this particular method of pill taking.

Long-term health benefits from using combined contraception include protection against ovarian and endometrial (womb lining) cancers.

Side Effects of Combined Contraception

Most of the side effects associated with combined contraception are temporary and will resolve within a few weeks. These include mood swings, nausea, bloating, breast tenderness and enlargement. More serious side effects, such as deep vein thrombosis, are rare. Occasionally, headaches can occur during the hormone-free interval. This is called oestrogen withdrawal, and can be improved by either changing to a preparation with a short hormone-free interval of four days, or else using combined contraception in a 'back to back' fashion (see above).

A long-term health risk associated with usage of combined contraception is a slight increase in breast cancer rates, which is not related to the number of years the woman used combined contraception. However, these findings are based on women who were using a much higher dose of oestrogen compared to the low dose hormones now prescribed. There is also an increase in cervical cancer rates, but it is still unclear as to whether combined contraception itself is a direct cause. Human papillomavirus (HPV) and smoking remain the biggest risk factors in the development of cervical cancer.

Progestogen-containing Contraception

Progestogens, as mentioned before, are artificial forms of progesterone, a hormone produced by the ovaries. It can be used in various forms and doses to provide varying degrees of contraception, depending on the needs of the woman. Progestogens are especially ideal for women who cannot use oestrogen-containing contraception. These include women with a history of blood clots themselves or a strong family history of blood clots, obese women, women with high blood pressure, diabetics, smokers over 35 years of age, women with certain types of severe migraine and women on certain medications, such as anti-epilepsy drugs.

Progestogens are available in several different forms, which are described in detail below.

Oral Form

This is otherwise known as the 'mini-pill'. This is an oral form of contraception which contains only progestogen; there is no oestrogen contained in it. There are currently two types of progestogen-only pills available in Ireland: Noriday and Cerazette.

Noriday (Norethisterone 350 mcg)

This acts mostly by making the cervical mucus thick and sticky, preventing sperm from reaching the egg to fertilise it. In very few patients it prevents ovulation. When used properly it can be approximately 95 per cent effective. However, because it does not stop ovulation in the majority of women, the failure rate is higher than that of the combined pill.

Cerazette (Desogestrel)

Cerazette is another form of progesterone-only contraceptive pill. However, it is different from Noriday in that it suppresses ovulation and, therefore, is a more reliable form of contraception. It also acts by thickening the cervical mucus, making it difficult for sperm to move upwards. When used properly for one year, less than one woman in one thousand will get pregnant using Cerazette. This is similar to the contraceptive cover provided by the combined oral contraceptives.

Taking the Mini-pill

The mini-pill is usually started on day 1 of a period. Breastfeeding women can start it at any time. If you start it on day 1 of your period, you are covered for contraception immediately. If you are starting it at any other time in your cycle, you can rely on it as contraception after seven tablets.

The pack of pills consists of 28 tablets, one of which is taken every day without a break. The pill must be taken at the same time every day; taking Noriday more than 3 hours late can reduce its efficacy; with Cerazette you have a 12-hour window during which you can take it. Your periods may continue to occur naturally while on the mini-pill or they may stop temporarily while you are taking it.

Side Effects

Most women will report some minor side effects when starting the mini-pill, almost all of which will resolve themselves quickly. These include breast tenderness, mood swings, bloating and headaches. Irregular bleeding while on the mini-pill can persist for some months after starting it.

Injectable Medroxyprogesterone Acetate (Depo-Provera)

Depo-Provera is an injection form of progestogen contraception containing medroxyprogesterone acetate (MPA). It acts by suppressing ovulation, i.e. it prevents an egg from being released from the ovary. It also thickens the mucus produced by the cervix, therefore slowing and preventing the passage of sperm upwards.

Depo-Provera is one of the most reliable forms of contraception available. When used properly for one year, less than one in one thousand women will get pregnant. Depo-Provera is suitable for most women, and it is particularly useful for young women who need a very reliable form of contraception but who may struggle to remember to take a daily tablet.

Unwanted side effects include weight gain and irregular menstrual bleeding. Periods will stop temporarily in most women who use it.

The injection is administered by a doctor every twelve weeks into a muscle, usually in the buttock. Although this is a very reliable form of contraception there is a failure rate of three per one thousand if not used properly. If it is administered in the first seven days of your cycle, your contraceptive cover will start immediately; otherwise, it will not take effect for another seven days. Some studies have shown a small amount of bone density loss with continuous use of Depo-Provera for longer than a few years. It is recommended that your doctor order a bone density measurement if you wish to continue with Depo-Provera for longer than this. The bone density loss is reversible on stopping the injection. There can sometimes be a delay in the return of your natural period after you stop using Depo-Provera.

Progestogen Implants (Implanon)

This is an implant of progestogen, which is placed just under the skin by your doctor using local anaesthetic. It is a rod-shaped device, which you can easily feel beneath the skin. It releases a small dose of hormone daily for three years, and provides excellent contraception. Periods are temporarily stopped while using Implanon, and return quickly after removal. However, irregular bleeding can be a problem after the first year of use. The implant is removed by your doctor.

Intrauterine Contraception

There are two forms of intrauterine contraception available in Ireland – a copper-releasing coil (also known as an intrauterine device (IUD)) and a progestogen-releasing coil (also known as an intrauterine system (IUS)).

Copper-releasing Coil

The copper-releasing coil is an IUD which is inserted into the womb by your doctor and can remain there for up to ten years. Its exact mechanism of contraception is not completely understood. The tiny amount of copper released causes a small amount of inflammation inside the womb, which may prevent implantation. It also makes cervical mucus thicker and prevents the passage of sperm. IUDs are suitable for all women, but are more commonly used by women who have had children, as insertion is easier for them. The contra-ceptive failure rate is higher than that of the progestogen-releasing device, and there can be associated period pain and heavier bleed-ing. However, these coils do provide one of the few non-hormonal forms of contraception and, therefore, there is always a place for their use.

Progestogen-releasing Device

Mirena is the progestogen-releasing IUS device used in Ireland. This is a T-shaped device which is coated with progestogen. A small dose of hormone is released daily, and it can be used for up to five years. It is suitable for all women. Insertion is relatively simple but, like the copper coil, is favoured more by women with previous preg-nancies as insertion is easier. It provides contraception equal to that of female sterilisation. It is used for both contraception and the management of heavy periods. This is because the constant release of low dose hormone into the uterus or womb prevents the lining of the womb from building up excessively. This causes your periods to become progressively lighter over twelve months after insertion. Twenty per cent of Mirena users will have no periods at this point. Occasionally, side effects such as mood swings and acne are reported, but this is uncommon.

The Mirena is now the treatment most commonly used for women with heavy periods. It can also be used as part of HRT for women who need treatment for menopausal symptoms.

Emergency Contraception

There are currently three types of emergency contraception available in Ireland:

- Levonelle is a single-dose tablet of levonorgestrel, which is administered up to 72 hours after unprotected sex. It has few side effects, and it is not clear how it works. Its overall effectiveness is approximately 75 per cent, but it is more effective if taken within 24 hours of unprotected sex.
- The Copper T 380 coil can be used as emergency contraception, and is used up to five days after unprotected sex. It is then removed at the next period. Its effectiveness is 99 per cent.
- EllaOne is the newest option available, and is a single-dose tablet which is effective for up to five days after unprotected sex. It works by delaying ovulation, therefore allowing sperm to die before ovulation takes place, preventing fertilisation.

Male Sterilisation (Vasectomy)

This is a permanent form of contraception and, although it can be reversed in some cases, it should be viewed as a permanent, irreversible form of contraception when being considered as an option.

How a Vasectomy Works

Sperm is produced in the testicles and stored in the epididymis. During ejaculation the sperm travel down a tube called the vas deferens to become part of the ejaculate. The procedure involves identifying the vas deferens in each scrotal sac and tying it off. These days it is usually done using a 'no scalpel' approach, where two tiny incisions are made in the scrotal skin, and the vas deferens is found and tied off. No sutures are required in the skin afterwards, and recovery is normally within a few days.

Key Points

- A wide variety of contraception options is available to suit most women's needs.
- Natural methods and barrier methods are hormone free but have a higher failure rate.
- The oral contraceptive pill is an effective and safe option that suits most women.
- Progesterone-only contraception offers more long-term contraception and is also suitable for women with epilepsy or a history of thrombosis.
- Intrauterine systems (IUSs) are particularly useful for women to help them space their pregnancies and when their family is complete.

9

Menstrual Cycle Problems

It can be difficult for women to know whether what they experience during their menstrual cycle is normal. It tends not to be discussed in great detail among friends and family! There is a huge variability in what a menstrual cycle should be, so quite often women feel that what they experience may not be the same as everyone else, when in fact it is normal and unique to them. I have outlined some of the more common period problems that women experience, with some guidelines as to what is considered normal.

The Menstrual Cycle

The menstrual cycle is the body's way of preparing for pregnancy. For the first half of the cycle, the lining of the womb, or endometrium, is thickening in preparation for implantation by an embryo. Ovulation then takes place, and if no fertilisation occurs, hormonal changes allow for the endometrium to start shedding, which is the period. The blood travels down through the cervix and into the vagina.

A 'normal' period is considered to be one that lasts for two to seven days, with a need to change pads or tampons no more frequently than once every couple of hours. The length of a cycle, i.e. counting from the first day of bleeding (day 1) to day 1 of your next period, can range from 21 to 45 days, depending on your age. In adults the normal length of a menstrual cycle ranges from 21 to 35 days, whereas in teenagers menstrual cycles can be as long as 42 days.

Female Reproductive System

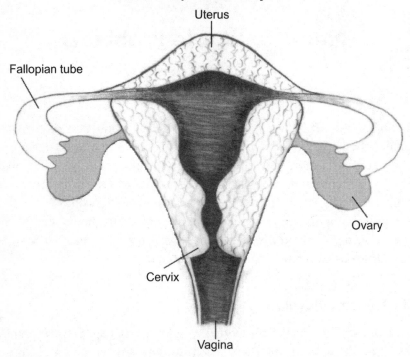

Heavy Periods

Heavy periods used to be defined as a certain amount of blood lost during each period, but more recently the definition has been changed to include the widespread impact which heavy periods can have on every aspect of a woman's life, i.e. excessive menstrual blood loss which interferes with a woman's physical, emotional, social and material quality of life.

Approximately 5 per cent of women aged between 30 to 49 years attend their doctors each year with heavy periods, but the actual percentage of women with heavy periods is thought to be higher – about 9 to 14 per cent worldwide. Heavy periods account for between 10 and 15 per cent of all anaemias. Women with heavy periods usually pass blood clots during their heaviest days, and some will experience flooding, whereby they pass a lot of blood suddenly on standing up or getting out of bed. For some women, pain may be a feature of their heavy periods, but for most the bleeding is painless. However, in a lot of cases the severity of bleeding means that for a certain time during their period they are confined to home.

Causes of Heavy Periods

The most common cause of heavy periods is called dysfunctional uterine bleeding. This is diagnosed when all other causes have been ruled out, and accounts for six out of ten cases. It is due to local changes within the endometrium. Other causes include fibroids, which are benign growths within the womb. This accounts for 10 per cent of cases. Cancer of the endometrium is a rare cause of heavy periods, as are clotting problems, which usually run in families and are picked up at a much earlier age, close to the onset of periods.

Diagnosing Heavy Periods

Your doctor should ask for a detailed history of your menstrual cycles and conduct a physical examination. They may notice signs of anaemia. Blood tests may be helpful to look for anaemia or low iron levels and, in some cases, thyroid function may be checked. If heavy bleeding has been a problem from the onset of your periods, a clotting problem can be checked for using blood testing. A pelvic ultrasound can be helpful in finding a cause for heavy periods. In some cases a hysteroscopy is needed, which is a day case procedure under anaesthetic where the lining of the womb is inspected using a tiny camera introduced through the cervix, and biopsies or tiny pieces of endometrium can be taken. This tends to be used for women aged over 45, who are at a slightly increased risk of endometrial cancer than younger women.

Treatment Options for Heavy Periods

Medication

Medication is used to control heavy periods when there is no significant problem detected inside the womb, such as very large fibroids. Some medications are used continuously; others are used only during your period.

Mirena Coil

This medicated device has become the mainstay in the treatment of heavy periods. It is a small, T-shaped device which is coated in the progesterone hormone and placed inside the cavity of the womb. It releases a tiny dose of hormone every day into the endometrium, which prevents it from growing excessively. It is easily inserted without anaesthetic in the doctor's surgery, and lasts for five years. It is also an excellent method of contraception.

Women should be told in advance that irregular bleeding for up to six months can occur after insertion of the coil, although the bleeding is usually very light. Side effects include acne, headache and breast tenderness, most of which only last a few weeks.

Tranexamic Acid (Cyklokapron)

Tranexamic acid is a non-hormonal treatment option for the management of heavy periods. It is taken as a tablet on the heaviest menstrual flow days. Studies show up to a 60 per cent improvement in blood loss. Side effects include gastrointestinal upset, and it should not be used in women with a personal or family history of blood clots.

Mefanamic Acid

This is another non-hormonal option for women. Mefanamic acid (Ponstan) is used on the heaviest days of menstrual flow. This has a 20 to 50 per cent reduction in menstrual flow, and for women who experience pain in association with their periods, this may be a preferred treatment option.

The Oral Contraceptive Pill

The combined oral contraceptive can be used with good effect. If you are over 35 you can safely use the oral contraceptive pill if you are of normal weight and a non-smoker. Qlaira is an oral contraceptive pill which is recommended as a treatment for heavy periods as well as for contraception. Shortening the pill-free interval of seven days helps to reduce blood loss. Yaz has 24 active pills, with a 4-day interval, which can be helpful.

These treatments should be stopped after three cycles if symptoms have not improved.

Norethisterone (Primolut N)

This hormone used to be a popular treatment for heavy periods before the Mirena coil was introduced. It is less commonly used now, but it can be used very effectively in a woman who is having a very prolonged period, as it stops it within a few days.

Surgery

In women who have heavy periods due to large fibroids and other significant symptoms, such as painful periods or pressure symptoms (e.g. on the bladder), surgery should be considered as a possible treatment.

Uterine Artery Embolisation

This is recommended for certain women with heavy periods associated with large fibroids. It is particularly suitable for women who have not finished having children, or who have yet to start a family. The blood vessel to the fibroid is permanently shut off, causing it to shrink completely. This is done under x-ray guidance through a vein in the groin.

Endometrial Ablation

This can be considered in women who have a slightly enlarged womb due to fibroids. Under general anaesthetic the endometrium is permanently removed while having a hysteroscopy. Pregnancy is not possible after this surgery, so tying the fallopian tubes is usually recommended at the same time.

Myomectomy

This is the removal of the fibroids by opening up the womb directly.

Hysterectomy

This is the removal of the womb and is a much less common procedure nowadays due to both the development of the Mirena coil and also less invasive surgery, such as ablation or embolisation. If a hysterectomy is necessary, a hysterectomy done through the vagina is better in terms of less complications and speed of recovery for the patient. It is also preferred to leave the ovaries behind at the time of surgery, provided they look normal. This allows the patient to maintain her female hormone levels.

Irregular Periods or Absent Periods

Definition

The medical terms for irregular periods and absent periods are oligomenorrhoea and amenorrhoea respectively. Oligomenorrhoea is defined as periods which are more than 35 days apart. Amenorrhoea can be primary or secondary. In other words, if you have not yet had a period by the age of 16 years, you have primary amenorrhoea. If you had previously been having periods, secondary amenorrhoea occurs when they stop for more than 90 days or the equivalent of three cycles in a row.

Primary Amenorrhoea

This is said to happen when a young girl has not had a natural period by the age of 16 years. There are several causes for this:

- Genetic problems
- Weight loss
- Extreme stress
- Over-exercising
- Chronic diseases

The most common cause for primary amenorrhoea is a genetic cause. In some young females, the ovaries fail very early in life and there are no eggs left in the ovaries; therefore, there is no hormone production. Another genetic condition is Turner syndrome, where one of the X chromosomes is missing and the ovaries never develop.

The production of hormones from the ovaries and, therefore, a menstrual cycle, is dependent on a complicated signalling system between the ovaries, the pituitary area of the brain and the hypo-thalamus, another portion of the brain. In the case of extreme weight loss, emotional or physical stress, over-exercising or chronic severe illness, the hypothalamus is affected, leading to the absence of periods.

A very rare cause of primary amenorrhoea is called androgen insensitivity, which is a genetic condition where an individual is born with XY chromosomes, in other words the genetic makeup of a male, but because of an inability of the body to recognise testosterone, the body does not develop as a male but as a female.

Secondary Amenorrhoea

When your periods have been absent for more than three consecutive cycles but they had previously been regular, further investigation is needed. Common reasons for this include:

- Pregnancy – this is the most common cause of secondary amenorrhoea.
- PCOS – this is the most common condition which causes amenorrhoea as a result of excessive testosterone levels (see below).
- Hypothalamic causes – these include excessive exercise, chronic severe illness, weight loss and physical or emotional stress.
- Prolactinoma – this is where a small tumour in the pituitary gland produces large amounts of prolactin which can shut down the menstrual cycle temporarily.
- Amenorrhoea after stopping the oral contraceptive pill – this is considered normal for up to three months after stopping the pill; after that investigations are required.
- Premature ovarian failure – this is the permanent stopping of periods under the age of 40.
- Hypothyroidism (underactive thyroid)

Diagnosis of Primary and Secondary Amenorrhoea

Your doctor should ask for a description of your symptoms. Lifestyle factors such as diet and exercise may be important, as well as symptoms like acne and excessive facial hair growth in the case of PCOS, or milky nipple discharge as seen with a prolactinoma. In the case of premature ovarian failure, menopausal symptoms may be present.

Blood tests include pituitary hormones, such as FSH, TSH and prolactin; ovarian hormones, such as oestradiol; and male hormones, such as testosterone and androstenedione. Other investigations may include a pelvic ultrasound, a CT scan or an MRI, depending on the cause.

Treatment of Primary and Secondary Amenorrhoea

The treatment for amenorrhoea varies, depending on the diagnosis and the desired outcome. If the cause of the amenorrhoea is due to hypothalamic causes, such as weight loss or over-exercising, then the underlying cause needs to be addressed.

In the case of PCOS, hormonal treatment may be needed to control the symptoms of excessive male hormone production. Medications such as cabergoline (Dostinex) can be used to reduce the overproduction of prolactin in the case of prolactinomas.

With premature ovarian failure, hormone replacement will greatly improve any unwanted symptoms associated with this hormone deficiency.

In some cases of amenorrhoea, a regular menstrual cycle can be achieved with ovulation in order to achieve pregnancy, using stimulation from prescribed medication (see Chapter 6).

Polycystic Ovarian Syndrome (PCOS)

PCOS deserves its own section, as it is such a common cause of irregular periods or absent periods. PCOS is a hormonal imbalance found in women which causes a variety of problems, including infertility, menstrual problems, heart disease and diabetes. It is seen in approximately 5 to 10 per cent of all women. PCOS appears to run in families. It is quite common to find that a patient with PCOS has a sister or mother with a similar clinical picture.

Symptoms and Causes of PCOS

Common symptoms of PCOS include:

- Infrequent or absent periods
- Acne
- Excessive dark hair growth on the face, back, stomach, thumbs or toes
- Weight gain or obesity
- High cholesterol
- High blood pressure
- Insulin resistance or type 2 diabetes

PCOS causes its associated problems because polycystic ovaries are unable to produce the normal levels of hormones required to release one egg at ovulation each month. Multiple cysts start to develop as normal at the beginning of the cycle, but none of them reach the critical size needed for ovulation. Therefore, progesterone is not produced and a bleed does not occur. The cysts formed also produce excessive amounts of male hormone. The cysts are rarely a cause for concern themselves but rather the hormonal imbalance that occurs with them.

Diagnosis of PCOS

PCOS is diagnosed in different ways. Your doctor will take a medical history and perform an examination. He or she will check your blood pressure and BMI. A pelvic ultrasound may be indicated. Blood tests to check for elevated male hormone levels should be done, as well as fasting cholesterol and blood glucose. The Rotterdam Criteria for diagnosing PCOS state that two out of the following three factors must be present to make the diagnosis:

- Irregular or absent periods
- Elevated levels of male hormone
- Appearance of PCOS on ovarian ultrasound

Treatment of PCOS

There is no cure for PCOS, and there is no one treatment plan for it. The appropriate treatment depends on what the patient's goal is – control of symptoms, optimising fertility or prevention of diabetes and heart disease. Listed below are some of the most commonly recommended treatment options for PCOS:

Lifestyle Changes

Obesity is very commonly associated with PCOS. Changing your diet and starting to exercise are vital parts of trying to tackle this difficult problem. Processed foods and foods with a high sugar content should be replaced with wholegrain foods, fruit and vegetables, and lean meat and fish. This reduces blood glucose levels and improves the way the body handles insulin, thereby reducing male hormone levels. Research has shown that even a 5 to 10 per cent reduction in body weight can restore regular periods and, therefore, ovulation.

Combined Oral Contraceptive Pill

This is used for women who have no desire to conceive at the time. It controls the irregular bleeding pattern and reduces the excessive hair growth. However, this only masks the symptoms of PCOS, which will recur when the pill is stopped. Typically, a combined pill which contains a progestogen with anti-androgen (anti-male hormone) properties is recommended, such as Dianette or Yasmin.

Diabetes Medications

A drug traditionally used in diabetes has proved somewhat useful in the management of PCOS. Metformin (Glucophage) lowers testosterone levels by changing the way insulin affects glucose levels. This slows hair growth, and ovulation may resume after a few months. It has also been shown to reduce body mass in some studies.

Fertility Medications

Absence of ovulation is the main reason for the infertility problems associated with PCOS. Clomiphene citrate (Clomid) is most commonly used but is associated with a risk of multiple pregnancies. Sometimes Clomid is used in conjunction with Glucophage, and this can allow lower levels of Clomid to be used. If treatment with Clomid is unsuccessful, then patients may be offered IVF.

Medication to Lower Male Hormones/Reduce Hair Growth

Drugs which lower male hormone levels are called anti-androgens. Aldosterone (Aldactone) reduces acne and hair growth. Anti-androgens can also be combined into oral contraceptives, such as Dianette, as mentioned above. Eflornithine (Vaniqa) is a cream which is successful in reducing hair growth in some women. Other measures such as electrolysis or laser hair removal can also work well in women with PCOS.

Surgery

This is sometimes used as a treatment option when medication has failed to induce ovulation. Laparoscopy is performed under anaesthetic, usually as a day case. Small holes are drilled into the surface of the ovary, and this temporarily reduces male hormone production.

Other Health Problems Associated With PCOS

Women with PCOS have greater chances of developing certain serious diseases than women without PCOS:

- As much as 50 per cent of women with PCOS will have developed diabetes or pre-diabetes before 40 years of age.
- Women with PCOS are five times more likely to develop heart disease.
- PCOS sufferers are more likely to have high cholesterol.
- They are more likely to have high blood pressure.
- The risk of cancer of the womb is greatly increased in women who are not having periods, due to the imbalance of hormones brought about by PCOS.

It is important to try and control PCOS at a younger age to prevent the development of future problems. It is essential to treat all the symptoms and not just focus on one, such as trying for a baby. Regular diabetes testing should be done. The importance of a healthy diet, regular exercise and not smoking cannot be underestimated in trying to prevent the aforementioned problems.

Premenstrual Syndrome (PMS)

PMS is a collection of various symptoms that occur during the second half of the menstrual cycle. These symptoms can be physical, psychological and emotional.

Signs and Symptoms of PMS

There are a large number of symptoms associated with PMS. Most women will be able to identify some of these symptoms which relate to them specifically. Nearly all women will be aware of some physical/psychological changes occurring during their menstrual cycle. These typically occur any time from mid-cycle onwards, and are relieved by the onset of the next period. Common symptoms include:

- Irritability
- Aggression
- Anxiety
- Exhaustion
- Tearfulness
- Alternating anger and sadness
- Depression
- Headaches and migraines
- Irritable bowel syndrome (IBS)
- Sweating
- Nausea
- Backache
- Abdominal bloating and fluid retention
- Pelvic pain
- Breast pain
- Appetite changes with food cravings

The symptoms often become gradually more severe as you get older, and often appear for the first time in your thirties and forties. Symptoms can worsen on approaching the menopause, and will disappear totally in postmenopausal women.

PMS Facts

Studies have shown that 20 to 30 per cent of women have significant PMS symptoms above and beyond the usual changes/discomfort suffered by menstruating women, and 2 to 5 per cent experience a severe form of PMS called premenstrual dysphoric disorder (PMDD).

Causes and Diagnosis of PMS

The exact cause of PMS is not known. Several studies have been carried out, but the results have been inconclusive. As a result, doctors have been unable to find a diagnostic test which can identify the condition. The condition is diagnosed by taking a careful history from the patient of her symptoms and the impact it has on her life and her relationships with others. Often, work is affected, as the woman struggles to cope. Keeping a menstrual diary and marking the onset of symptoms helps to confirm the diagnosis. It is generally believed that normal hormonal changes which occur as part of your cycle must contribute to the condition, with a possible interaction between these sex hormones and brain hormones, also called neurotransmitters.

PMS – What You Can Do

By reviewing your current lifestyle it may be possible to identify certain changes that can be made to reduce your level of PMS:

- Many people now lead very stressful lives. You should attempt to identify the areas of your life that are causing you stress and see if any changes can be made to alleviate these.
- Regular exercise has been shown to help both the physical and psychological causes of PMS.
- A good, balanced diet will help improve your overall health and hopefully reduce your levels of PMS. In particular, a low glycaemic index (GI) diet is recommended, as the slow release of sugars from low GI foods helps to combat the fluctuating blood sugar levels associated with PMS.
- Avoiding salt before a period can help alleviate symptoms.

- Availing of emotional support from family and friends can help with the emotional affects of PMS.
- Reducing your alcohol and caffeine intake and stopping smoking should help reduce PMS symptoms.

Other Treatment Options

Vitamin Supplements and Natural Therapies

Some studies have shown vitamin E, vitamin A, calcium and magnesium supplements to be useful in the treatment of PMS symptoms. However, other supplements, such as agnus castus and evening primrose oil, have not been shown to have any impact on PMS symptoms.

Anti-inflammatories

These are a group of medications used for pain relief and can be helpful in the relief of pelvic pain associated with PMS. Examples include mefanamic acid (Ponstan) and diclofenac (Difene).

The Oral Contraceptive Pill

The combined contraceptive pill is commonly used as the first line of treatment for PMS. Although it does not help every woman, it can be very effective. It works by stopping hormone production from the ovaries temporarily, therefore providing a constant steady level of female hormones released by the pill. In particular, preparations which shorten the pill-free interval, such as Yaz, can be very helpful.

Ovarian Suppressants

Danocrine (Danazol) is a powerful ovarian suppressant, which can be used in severe cases of PMS. The side effects are very marked and, therefore, it is not usually used for long periods. However, it can be useful to help diagnose severe PMS. GnRH agonists are a group of injectable drugs which also suppress the ovaries for several months at a time. Again, they cannot be used for prolonged periods of time, because of the risk of osteoporosis. However, they can be used in conjunction with oestrogen for longer periods.

Antidepressant Medication

Medical studies have shown that certain types of antidepressant medication, namely selective serotonin re-uptake inhibitors (SSRIs), have been successful in treating women who suffer from severe psychological symptoms associated with PMS for prolonged periods of time. These can be used either constantly throughout the month or just for the second half of the menstrual cycle, when the symptoms are usually most marked. Examples of these include Lustral and Prozac.

Painful Periods

The gynaecological term for painful periods is dysmenorrhoea. The pain is a result of cramps caused by contracting of the muscle within the wall of the uterus or womb. Certain chemicals called prostaglandins (also used to induce labour) are produced when the lining of the womb or endometrium is being shed, and these chemicals bring about the cramps. These chemicals are found in much higher levels in women who experience severe pain. The pain can be associated with nausea, upper leg and back pain, and vomiting in some cases. An assessment of the impact of the dysmenorrhoea on a woman's life should be taken into consideration, including days lost from work and so on.

Primary Dysmenorrhoea

Primary dysmenorrhoea refers to painful periods which have been a feature since shortly after a young girl has started having periods. Typically, the first few periods will be painless, and then the pain becomes a feature. The pain is usually seen after the onset of bleeding and is relieved within a few days.

Diagnosis and Treatment of Primary Dysmenorrhoea

The diagnosis is based mainly on the patient's history of painful periods starting within a year of the onset of menstruation, and the absence of other symptoms and signs suggestive of underlying gynaecological problems. The pain should also tend to be after the onset of the period, and should usually last for up to 72 hours only. The initial treatment of primary dysmenorrhoea should be either non-steroidal anti-inflammatories (NSAIDs) or the oral contraceptive pill.

NSAIDs

These should be used before the onset of bleeding, and continued for a few days afterwards. They are also more effective when taken as a regular medication (e.g. three times per day) rather than whenever the pain becomes intense. This way, the pain is better controlled.

Oral Contraceptive Pill

This works by reducing the amount of endometrium produced, which reduces the pain at the time of bleeding. Higher doses of oestrogen of between 30 and 35 mcg should be used rather than the very low dose pills which are adequate for contraception alone.

Often, both NSAIDs and the oral contraceptive pill are required to control pain.

Secondary Dysmenorrhoea

Secondary dysmenorrhoea is seen in women who have previously had little or no pain with their periods. It is usually caused by an underlying gynaecological problem. Typically the pain starts before the bleeding appears, and can persist right through the period. Indeed, pain can occur throughout the menstrual cycle for some women.

Common causes of secondary dysmenorrhoea include:

- Endometriosis – this is a condition where endometrium or womb lining is found in areas outside the womb, most commonly on the ovaries. With each period this tissue bleeds, leading to pain and eventually scar tissue.
- Adenomyosis – this is a condition where endometrium lies within the thick muscle layer of the womb. With menstruation, bleeding occurs in this layer, leading to swelling of the womb and pain.
- Pelvic inflammatory disease (PID) – this is a pelvic infection usually caused by a sexually transmitted infection, which can cause painful periods among other symptoms.
- Fibroids – benign or non-cancerous growths within the womb which can lead to painful and heavy periods.
- Intrauterine devices (IUDs) – these are usually inserted quite close to the onset of dysmenorrhoea.
- Endometrial polyps – these are benign overgrowths of endometrium.

Diagnosis and Treatment of Secondary Dysmenorrhoea

The diagnosis of secondary dysmenorrhoea also depends primarily on patient history and physical examination. Typically, it starts in women over the age of 25, and can begin at any time in the cycle after mid-cycle or ovulation. The pain usually precedes bleeding.

Physical examination will show an abnormality in 40 per cent of cases where there is a physical cause for the dysmenorrhoea. Some appropriate investigations may include pelvic ultrasound and hysterosalpingogram (HSG).

In severe cases laparoscopy may be needed. This is a keyhole surgery technique where a camera is inserted through the belly-button (umbilicus) to look for any abnormalities in the pelvis. This can also be combined with a procedure called ablation, where a laser is used to burn away any spots of endometriosis present. Laparoscopy tends to be reserved for women who have not responded to medication. For causes other than endometriosis the treatment will depend on the underlying cause.

Endometriosis

Endometriosis is a condition where small pieces of the lining of the womb or endometrium are found outside the womb. On a monthly basis the endometrium thickens and then sheds in the form of a period. With endometriosis, these spots of endometrium outside the womb thicken and then shed into the pelvis, causing pain, swelling and potential scarring. Endometriosis is found primarily on the ovaries, fallopian tubes, bladder or bowel.

Symptoms

Typical symptoms of endometriosis include:

- Painful periods
- Pain often starts before the bleeding
- Pain in the lower back, lower abdomen or tummy
- Pain during sex
- Bleeding between periods
- Fertility problems

Diagnosis and Treatment

To diagnose endometriosis, a laparoscopy is performed. This is a procedure carried out under anaesthetic whereby the pelvis is examined directly. If endometriosis is found, it can be treated at the same time by using an electric current to destroy the small areas of endometriosis. Non-surgical treatments include the oral contraceptive pill and the intrauterine system (IUS). The oral contraceptive pill can also be used for three packs in a row continuously to reduce the number of bleeds. Non-steroidal anti-inflammatory drugs (NSAIDs) can also be useful for reducing the pain associated with endometriosis. Endometriosis is not curable, but depending on the symptoms associated with it, such as pain or infertility, appropriate treatment can be very helpful.

Bleeding Between Periods

Bleeding between periods or intermenstrual bleeding is bleeding which occurs at times in the cycle other than at the time of the period. There are many causes for this:

- Hormonal conditions, such as PCOS
- Early pregnancy or a miscarriage
- Uterine fibroids
- Endometrial cancer
- Cancer of the cervix
- Trauma to the vagina, such as from sexual intercourse
- Pelvic infection, usually due to sexually transmitted infections such as chlamydia
- Endometriosis
- Oral contraceptives, either when taken regularly or especially if one or two have been missed

Other causes are also possible. In some cases, no cause can be found.

Diagnosis and Treatment of Intermenstrual Bleeding

The following information or details may help your doctor discover the cause of your bleeding:

- A description of your normal menstrual cycle
- Information about when the irregular bleeding started and how much bleeding there has been
- Date of the last normal period
- Date of the last cervical smear
- Any new sexual partners or unprotected sex
- Details of whether you are sexually active and, if so, the type of birth control you use
- Previous episodes of intermenstrual bleeding
- Pain or cramps associated with the bleeding
- Recent injuries to the pelvic area
- Other symptoms, such as weight loss, nausea or fever

A physical examination will help the doctor ascertain the extent of the bleeding and may be all that is needed in terms of investigations. A pregnancy test and a blood count to check if a lot of blood has been lost may also be appropriate. Inspection of the cervix will help to rule out cervical cancer as a cause, and screening for STIs may be necessary. A pelvic ultrasound may be required. The treatment needed, if any, will mainly depend on the underlying cause found.

Ovarian Cysts

An ovarian cyst is a fluid-filled bag either within or on the surface of an ovary. They are extremely common due to the ongoing activity of the ovaries during a woman's reproductive life. They usually cause no symptoms at all and resolve themselves without any treatment. However, in some cases they can cause quite severe symptoms and may need to be removed. The vast majority of ovarian cysts occur in premenopausal women.

Signs and Symptoms of Ovarian Cysts

Symptoms associated with an ovarian cyst include pelvic pain (usually one-sided), irregular vaginal bleeding, pain during sex, pressure symptoms, such as more frequent passing of urine, pain passing a bowel motion, or a feeling of fullness in the lower abdomen.

Types of Ovarian Cysts

Ovarian cysts can come in any of the following forms:

- Functional – these are simple cysts that develop as a result of ovarian activity. They are formed by a collection of fluid which happens at the exact spot where an egg is to be released from the surface of the ovary. These cysts are filled with clear fluid.
- Dermoid – this type of cyst is also known as a teratoma and contains cells from different parts of the body. A dermoid cyst can contain hair, teeth and cartilage. These cysts contain solid and fluid components.
- Cystadenoma – this is a cyst which can develop from ovarian tissue itself.
- Endometrioma – this is also known as a chocolate cyst. These cysts are seen with endometriosis, where cysts form which are filled with blood.

Diagnosis of Ovarian Cysts

An ovarian cyst can be diagnosed by pelvic examination if it is sufficiently large. Pelvic ultrasound is used to accurately measure the size of the cyst and to establish what type of cyst is present. Laparoscopy is occasionally used to see the cyst directly, and remove it at the same time if necessary. Sometimes in postmenopausal women a blood test called CA 125 can be done to check whether the cyst could be cancerous.

Treatment of Ovarian Cysts

Treatment of an ovarian cyst depends on the size of the cyst, the type of cyst it appears to be on ultrasound, and the presence of any symptoms, such as pain. The vast majority of cysts are monitored closely with ultrasound if they are not causing symptoms and are filled with fluid only. The oral contraceptive pill can be used to reduce the chances of further cysts developing. If the cyst contains solid matter within it, if it is larger than 5 cm in diameter, or if it is causing symptoms, your doctor may recommend removing the cyst using a laparoscopic procedure. Very occasionally the ovary itself needs to be removed if the cyst has caused significant damage to it.

Uterine Fibroids

These are benign growths which can develop in the muscle layer of the uterus. It is estimated that at least 50 per cent of all women have fibroids, but the vast majority of fibroids cause no problems. They have almost no tendency to become cancerous. They are rarely a problem for women after the menopause, as the fibroids grow in response to female hormones, and correspondingly shrink after hormone production stops at the menopause.

Symptoms of Uterine Fibroids

The symptoms associated with fibroids depend on the location of the growths. If they are located inside the uterus, heavy periods and difficulty conceiving are more common symptoms. If the fibroid is located on the outside of the uterus, pressure symptoms, such as frequent urination and back ache, may be present.

Diagnosis and Treatment of Uterine Fibroids

Fibroids may be detected upon examination by your doctor, but an ultrasound will pinpoint the exact location of the fibroid. As mentioned above, the vast majority of fibroids require no treatment. However, if they are causing symptoms, a number of treatments are available, varying from medication, minimally invasive techniques and surgery if necessary.

Key Points

- Heavy periods can adversely affect every aspect of a woman's life.
- The most common cause is hormonal imbalance, which is normal as you get older.
- Most cases of heavy periods can be treated using medication, in particular an intrauterine system (IUS), such as the Mirena coil.
- The oral contraceptive pill and NSAIDs are used very effectively to treat painful periods.
- PMS is usually successfully treated with the oral contraceptive pill but other treatment options are also available.
- PCOS is a very common cause of irregular periods.

10

Urinary and Genital Problems

Pelvic Floor Damage

The pelvic floor is the term given to a large group of muscles and tissues which lie in a horizontal plane in the pelvis, supporting the pelvic organs. These muscles are very strong and act as a sling to hold up the rectum, uterus and bladder. They can be damaged in pregnancy, vaginal delivery of a baby, surgery and radiotherapy treatment. It is estimated that approximately one-third of all women will have a pelvic floor disorder during their lifetime. The consequences of pelvic floor damage can be:

- Utero-vaginal prolapse
- Bladder prolapse
- Bowel prolapse

Utero-vaginal Prolapse

This is when the womb or uterus falls down into the vagina, because of weakened muscles which had previously kept it up above the vagina. Causes apart from pregnancy and childbirth include repeated strain on the muscles, such as a chronic cough with smokers, chronic constipation, loss of oestrogen after the menopause, and obesity.

Symptoms of Utero-vaginal Prolapse

Symptoms of utero-vaginal prolapse include:

- A sensation of something coming down inside the vagina, especially after standing for some time
- Urinary difficulty or incontinence
- A lump that can be felt at the vaginal opening
- Difficulty passing a bowel motion
- Low back pain
- Discomfort during sex

Diagnosis of Utero-vaginal Prolapse

There are varying degrees of prolapse, ranging from a slight dropping down of the cervix within the vagina, through to the whole cervix and womb being outside the vagina (also known as procidentia). Examination by your doctor is sufficient to make the diagnosis. Your doctor may want to examine you while lying and standing, and may ask you to bear down as if trying to pass a bowel motion. This helps to demonstrate the prolapse.

How to Treat Utero-vaginal Prolapse

Utero-vaginal prolapse does not necessarily require any treatment if it is not causing any significant symptoms. In mild cases some physiotherapy to strengthen the pelvic floor muscles, stopping smoking or weight loss is enough to treat the prolapse. The use of vaginal oestrogen in the form of a cream or tablet can help with local symptoms.

In more severe cases a plastic device can be inserted into the vagina by your doctor, which helps to support the womb and improve the symptoms of pressure caused by the prolapse. These are called ring pessaries and are changed every few months by your doctor. They provide a reasonable alternative to surgery, especially in older women who are reluctant to undergo a procedure.

For younger women surgery may be more appropriate if the symptoms are very marked. However, it is not usually recommended to have surgery to repair a prolapse if the woman has not finished having children. Usually, the surgeon will perform a vaginal hysterectomy, and may repair any other prolapse present at the same time, such as a cystocele or rectocele (see below). In rare cases where the woman has not finished having children a procedure which suspends the uterus using a synthetic sling can be used.

Cystocele (Bladder Prolapse)

This is a prolapse of the bladder into the vagina, leading to a ballooning of the front wall of the vagina. This is due to a weakness in the supportive tissues which lie between the bladder and the vagina. The causes of cystocele are similar to those of a uterine prolapse, i.e. pregnancy and vaginal childbirth, repeated straining, menopause and obesity. Cystocele is also seen more commonly in women who have had a hysterectomy, as the presence of the womb provides added support to the vaginal walls.

Signs and Symptoms of Cystocele

Symptoms of cystocele include:

- A sensation of something in the vagina
- A sensation of incomplete emptying of your bladder
- Recurrent urinary infections
- Leaking of urine with coughing or sneezing
- A lump which can be felt at the vaginal opening

Diagnosis and Treatment of Cystocele

The diagnosis of a cystocele is made by examination alone, and your doctor may want you to cough while examining you, to demonstrate any urine leakage.

Treatment of a cystocele is similar to that of a uterine prolapse. In mild cases pelvic floor exercises, local oestrogen treatment and weight loss may be sufficient. With larger cystoceles, ring pessaries or surgery are usually suggested, depending on the age and the health of the woman. Surgery is performed through the vagina and consists of opening up the front wall of the vagina, strengthening the wall, removing any excess tissue and closing it again. Recovery time from the procedure is reasonably quick, and most patients are home within a few days.

Rectocele (Rectal Prolapse)

This is a prolapse of the rectum into the vagina, ballooning forward and pushing on the back wall of the vagina. It is due to a weakness in the tissues that lie between the rectum and vagina. The causes include pregnancy and childbirth, obesity, menopause and chronic constipation. A less common form of rectal prolapse is an enterocele, where loops of small bowel prolapse at the top of the vagina, causing the back wall of the vagina to bulge at the top near the cervix. Both rectoceles and enteroceles are dignosed on examination of the vagina by your doctor.

Signs and Symptoms of Rectocele

Symptoms of a rectocele include:

- A feeling of fullness in the vagina
- A feeling of incomplete emptying of the rectum after finishing a bowel motion

- Difficulty emptying the rectum during a bowel motion; some women find that by pressing on the back wall of the vagina with their finger, this helps to complete the bowel motion.

Treatment of Rectocele

Rectoceles can be managed with physiotherapy or with surgery, where the back wall of the vagina is opened, reinforced and closed again while removing any excess tissue which has become stretched by the prolapse.

Urinary Incontinence

Incontinence is defined as the involuntary loss of urine and is thought to be very much more common than statistics would suggest. Women just do not want to talk about this embarrassing problem to their doctor, or they may feel that there are no treatment options available other than surgery. The truth is about 70 per cent of all cases of female incontinence can be significantly improved without resorting to surgery.

In order to understand the reasons behind the various forms of incontinence, the mechanism of urination should be explained. Urine is produced by the kidneys and transported to the bladder via two small tubes called the ureters. The bladder is a muscular bag, from which emerges a tube called the urethra, through which urine is passed while urinating. The bladder and urethra is supported by the powerful pelvic floor muscles. When the bladder is sufficiently full, a message is sent to the brain to go to the toilet. Once in the toilet and ready to urinate, the brain sends a message to the muscles surrounding the urethra to relax, allowing urine to leave the bladder. The bladder muscle contracts, pushing the urine into the urethra. Incontinence comes about when one of the mechanisms of urinating is not functioning correctly.

Types of Incontinence

There are several types of incontinence, which are discussed below.

Stress Incontinence

This is the type of urinary incontinence classically associated with pregnancy and childbirth. Typically, a woman who has had several vaginal deliveries (possibly with one or two heavy babies at birth) leaks urine when coughing, laughing or sneezing. Stress incontinence comes about when the pelvic floor has been weakened, leading to reduced support for the urethra and the lower end of the urethra (bladder neck). During activities such as coughing and sneezing, the pressure exerted on the bladder is greater than the pressure keeping the urethra closed, and urine is leaked involuntarily.

Stress incontinence is more likely to be seen:

- After childbirth
- With increased pressure on the abdominal area, e.g. in pregnancy or very obese women
- With postmenopausal women

Urge Incontinence

This type of incontinence is brought about by excessive activity of the bladder muscle. This causes multiple messages to be sent to the brain indicating that urination needs to happen urgently when in fact the bladder may not contain much urine at all. This leads to a marked feeling of urgency, accompanied by either incontinence at the same time or shortly after. Often patients describe coming home, opening their front door, moving towards the bathroom but wetting themselves before reaching it. Likewise, a running tap may cause them to leak urine. It is not fully understood why urge incontinence occurs. Caffeinated drinks, such as coffee, tea or cola, can contribute to the problem by irritating the bladder. In rare cases it can be associated with other illnesses, such as multiple sclerosis, Parkinson's disease and diabetes. The term 'urge incontinence' is often used interchangeably with 'overactive bladder' (OAB), which is a frequent urge to urinate brought about by overactivity of the bladder muscles, but without actual incontinence.

Mixed Incontinence

This is the most common form of urinary incontinence found in women, whereby they are having symptoms of both stress and urge incontinence. Pure stress incontinence or pure urge incontinence is rarely seen.

Functional Incontinence

This is the type of incontinence seen when medical conditions interfere with a woman's ability to reach a toilet when needed. Examples may include Alzheimer's disease, arthritis or being wheelchair bound.

Diagnosis of Urinary Incontinence

The first step in diagnosing urinary incontinence is to see your doctor. They will ask you various questions regarding the pattern of your toilet habits and urine leakage. A full medical history, current medications and a history of your fluid intake should be taken. Your doctor may ask you to keep a diary of all urination and the volumes of urine produced over a 24-hour period. This can sometimes help to figure out which kind of incontinence you have. A pelvic examination can help to diagnose any growths within the pelvis which may be causing your incontinence, and evidence of prolapse as described above would suggest a pelvic floor weakness which may be responsible for the incontinence.

Other investigations which may be necessary include the following:

- A urine sample should be checked for any evidence of infection. Your doctor may be able to check for infection at their own surgery or clinic, or a sample might be sent to the laboratory for a closer inspection. Urine infection can cause temporary incontinence.
- Urodynamics is the investigation which is most helpful in deciphering which kind of incontinence is present. This involves measuring the pressure in the bladder while the bladder is slowly filled with water.
- Cystoscopy is where the doctor inspects the bladder using a small tube containing a camera.

Treatment Options

What Can I Do?

There is good evidence to suggest that by sticking to the following self-help measures, 70 per cent of women will improve their incontinence to such a degree that they will not require any further intervention:

- If you are overweight, weight loss will improve the degree of incontinence you are experiencing.
- Reducing or avoiding tea, coffee, fizzy drinks and alcohol can be helpful, as these are all bladder stimulants. Acidic fruit and vegetables, including oranges and tomatoes, will irritate the bladder, as will spicy foods. Reducing total daily fluid intake to 1 litre per 24 hours will also help. If nocturia – or night-time toilet trips – is a big feature of the problem, the last fluid intake should be no later than 6.00 p.m.

- For both stress and urge incontinence changing your behaviour can have a positive response. Firstly, bladder drill or training, also known as timed voiding, can be introduced. This involves lengthening the time between toilet trips by a few minutes every day. By suppressing the urge to void urine, the bladder can be trained to relax for increasingly longer periods of time. This should be preceded by a voiding diary, as this will help to identify periods during the day when toilet trips are at their most frequent.

- Pelvic floor exercises can help both types of incontinence. This involves repetitive squeezing of the pelvic floor which slowly strengthens the muscles, increasing the support within the pelvis. These should be done initially while lying on your back with your knees bent and both feet flat on the floor. Sometimes it is hard to isolate these muscles, and you end up squeezing every muscle in your bottom and legs instead of the ones that count. To help you isolate the pelvic floor it helps to imagine that you are pulling up a zip which starts at the bottom of the vagina and finishes at your belly button. You should hold it for 3 seconds then release for 3 seconds. You should be aiming to build this up to three sets of ten squeezes, taking about 5 minutes. Results should be seen within a few weeks. As you get stronger at the exercises, you can do them sitting upright, which makes them a little more difficult as you are working against gravity. If you are struggling with the exercises you may need the help of a physiotherapist who can help you identify the exact muscles you should be squeezing.

- If you are on any medications for high blood pressure or ankle swelling this may not be helping your urinary symptoms, because they increase the volume of urine produced. You should talk to your doctor about possibly changing medication.

Medication for Urge Incontinence

If treatments like bladder drill don't work your doctor may suggest trying medication for urge incontinence of overactive bladder. This works on the bladder muscle, stopping it from twitching as much and relieving the sense of urge and the incontinence. These drugs are called antimuscarinics, and should be started initially at a relatively low dose to try to avoid side effects, which include dry mouth, dizziness, constipation, wind, drowsiness and dry eyes.

Surgery for Stress Incontinence

Surgery for stress incontinence is only required for a small number of patients, as pelvic floor exercises and weight loss will improve the incontinence very effectively in the majority of women. Nevertheless, for some women, despite their best efforts, the incontinence continues to be a huge problem and for them surgery is a good option. The most popular option now is called a sling procedure. This is a procedure done through the vagina, where a piece of tape is inserted under the neck of the bladder and pulled upwards to increase the support of the bladder neck and dramatically reduce or even eliminate stress incontinence. It is a relatively simple procedure, which is very effective, and the woman is usually back to normal within a day or two. Success rates are as high as 80 to 90 per cent.

Hormonal Treatments

For older women, being postmenopausal means that the tissues in the genital area have become thinned and weakened from a lack of oestrogen. This can contribute to urinary symptoms such as urgency and urinary frequency. For these women a course of vaginal oestrogen will restore the vaginal and urethral area and their distressing symptoms can often be greatly relieved. Vagifem is a vaginal tablet which can be easily inserted into the vagina at night twice a week for a few months.

Urinary Tract Infections (UTIs)

This is a very common condition in women of all ages. It is estimated that 60 per cent of all women will experience a UTI during their lifetime. They are also much more common in women than in men, the reasons for which are listed below.

A UTI is any infection of the urinary tract. The urinary tract consists of two kidneys, from which lead two tubes called the ureters. These drain into the bladder, and the urethra is the tube leading from the lower end of the bladder to the area just above the vaginal opening.

Infection of the bladder and urethra, known as cystitis and urethritis respectively, are the most common forms of UTIs. Infection of the kidneys is called pyelonephritis and usually affects only one kidney at a time. This is actually relatively uncommon. Women will often describe themselves as suffering from a 'kidney infection' when in fact they have a bladder infection.

As much as 80 per cent of UTIs are caused by E coli, a bacterium found in the colon.

Symptoms of UTIs

The symptoms of a UTI depend on the area of the urinary tract affected:

- Cystitis – this is marked by lower abdominal pain, a sensation of pressure in the pelvis with an increased urge to urinate, frequent painful urination and the presence of blood visible in your urine.
- Pyelonephritis – symptoms include high fever, upper back or side pain, nausea, vomiting and chills.
- Urethritis – the most common symptom of urethritis is a burning sensation when urinating. The urine may also be noted to have a strong smell or appear cloudy.

Female Urinary System

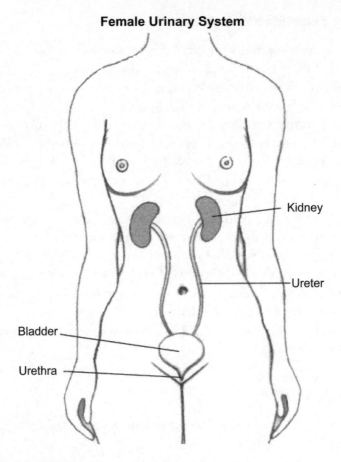

Kidney

Ureter

Bladder

Urethra

Why Do They Happen?

There are several reasons why women get UTIs:

- Our anatomy – women have a short urethra, which means that bacteria have a short distance to travel and the urinary tract is more vulnerable to infection entering from outside the body.
- Sexual activity – having sex encourages the travel of bacteria up the urethra into the bladder.

- Use of diaphragms as a form of contraception can increase your risk of getting a UTI.
- Being postmenopausal – the lack of oestrogen seen with the menopausal state leaves the urinary tract more susceptible to infection.
- Congenital abnormalities of the urinary tract – babies born with abnormalities of the urinary tract will be more likely to develop infection.
- Using urinary catheters – women who need to place a tube or catheter into their own bladders to empty the bladder artificially will be more likely to introduce infection.
- Pregnancy – the hormone progesterone which is produced in large amounts during pregnancy causes the urinary tract to dilate or open up, leading to an increased risk of infection.

Diagnosis of a UTI

Infection of the urinary tract is usually easy to diagnose in adult women. A history from the patient usually points towards a urinary infection. Your doctor may also examine a specimen of your urine immediately by using a dipstick. This can detect some signs of infection in the urine but is not always able to diagnose all infections. The sample of urine should be sent to the local laboratory if possible to look for any bacteria that may be present. The laboratory will also indicate the best antibiotic treatment necessary to clear the infection. In rare cases where recurrent infection is present you may be referred for a cystoscopy, which is a long, thin tube containing a camera which examines the bladder carefully.

Treatment of UTIs

Treatment of a UTI usually involves antibiotics. The most common ones used include ampicillin, nitrofurantoin and trimethoprim. In the case of pyelonephritis, or infection of the kidneys, admission to hospital and intravenous antibiotics may be required.

Potassium citrate sachets are available over the counter in pharmacies for the relief of cystitis and urethritis symptoms. The potassium citrate neutralises the acidity of the urine, which relieves symptoms. However, it is only recommended for 48-hour use, after which time it is advisable to see your doctor.

It is also advisable to increase your intake of water, as this often helps to reduce symptoms. Tea, coffee and alcohol can worsen cystitis symptoms, so it is best to reduce your intake of these or to eliminate them while you are symptomatic.

Prevention of UTIs

Here are a few tips to remember:
- Drink plenty of water during the day, allowing any bacteria to get flushed away because of frequent urination.
- Urinate within 30 minutes of sexual intercourse.
- Always wipe from front to back after going to the toilet.
- Do not use feminine products in the genital area.

Recurrent UTIs

This is defined as three or more documented UTIs in one year. These are usually related to sexual activity and do not necessarily require specialist investigation. Treatment includes the general measures listed above, as well as possibly taking an antibiotic tablet at night for prolonged periods of up to six months. Other treatments involve taking a single antibiotic tablet after sexual intercourse, which can often be all that is needed.

Age-related Vaginal Changes and Urogenital Atrophy

Thinning and inflammation of the skin in the genital area, also known as urogenital atrophy, occurs when oestrogen levels drop at the time of the menopause. While it most commonly occurs around the time of the menopause, it can also be seen in women who are breastfeeding or have other conditions where oestrogen levels are very low. Some of these include:

- Breastfeeding
- After undergoing chemotherapy for cancer
- After pelvic radiotherapy for cancer
- While using certain medications to treat breast cancer

How Common Is Urogenital Atrophy?

Vaginal problems associated with the menopause are extremely common, with an estimated 50 per cent of all women experiencing them. However, it is often not reported by the patient because of embarrassment.

Signs and Symptoms of Urogenital Atrophy

Oestrogen is found in many parts of the genital area and, therefore, when the levels drop the effects of this are seen in several different areas, leading to a variety of often debilitating symptoms. Mucus production is usually greatly reduced, and the skin and tissues of the vagina become thinner. Glycogen production is also reduced, as a result of reduced oestrogen. Glycogen helps to protect the vagina from infection, so an increase in bacterial infections can be seen with urogenital atrophy. It should be noted that these symptoms affect women who are not sexually active as well as those who are; for some, the vaginal symptoms are severe and can include:

- Vaginal dryness
- Vaginal burning
- Vaginal itching
- Shortening and tightening of the vaginal canal

- Increased incidence of urinary tract infections
- Soreness associated with sex
- Burning with urination
- Urgency with urination
- Urinary incontinence
- Increase in vaginal infections

Risk Factors for Urogenital Atrophy

Although urogenital atrophy is common to all women, there are some factors which seem to make women more likely to have problems. These include:

- A history of smoking – it is well recognised that women who smoke are more likely to have an earlier menopause and reduced hormone levels.
- Women who are not regularly sexually active – having regular sex seems to protect somewhat against urogenital atrophy.
- Women who have never had a vaginal delivery are more likely to experience vaginal problems as they age.

Diagnosis and Treatment of Urogenital Atrophy

Diagnosis of urogenital atrophy involves taking a history of symptoms from the patient, as well as a genital examination. The doctor will usually find paler labia, with some areas of redness inside the vagina which bleed easily on examination. In some cases examining the vagina is not possible due to pain or soreness. In women with more marked symptoms, hormonal treatment can be used with great success. In the case of mild symptoms, a vaginal moisturiser or lubricant may be sufficient to keep the area comfortable. More detailed treatment options are provided below.

Vaginal Oestrogen

In Ireland the only vaginal oestrogen treatment available is in the form of a tablet (Vagifem). Vaginal oestrogen is also available in creams and insertable rings, but there is no real difference between them in terms of effectiveness. There is minimal if any absorption into the bloodstream and, therefore, it is not classified as hormone replacement therapy (HRT). It can thus be used indefinitely without concern.

Hormone Replacement Therapy (HRT)

This can be used in cases where other menopausal symptoms, such as flushes and sweats, are present in addition to vaginal symptoms.

Vaginal Moisturisers

These products, such as Replens, can be useful in mild cases.

Lubricants

Oil-based lubricants, such as Sylk, are very helpful in postmenopausal women.

Key Points

- Prolapse as a result of pelvic floor damage is very common in women who have given birth, but it only requires treatment if it is causing significant symptoms.
- There are two types of incontinence – stress and urge.
- Almost 70 per cent of stress incontinence can be successfully treated with physiotherapy.
- Urinary tract infections (UTIs) are a common problem in women.
- Recurrent UTIs can be treated with low-dose antibiotics for three to six months.

11

Osteoporosis

Osteoporosis is the most common bone disease in women. It is much more common than you might think, affecting one in three women over the age of 50. It does not cause symptoms, so you may not know you have it until you break a bone, by which time the disease is quite advanced. The good news is that it can be detected early before it becomes severe enough to cause major problems, and there are very successful treatments available to stop any further bone disease, and also to rebuild some strength back into your bones. Changing your lifestyle now can help in a huge way to stop you from developing this serious disease later in life.

Causes of Osteoporosis

Our bones are made up of a complicated crisscross pattern of strong bands inside a hard outer shell. In between the crisscross pattern are collagen and calcium, among other materials, filling in the gaps. In healthy, strong bones there are very few gaps; in weaker bones there are much larger gaps within the bone, making them more likely to break.

There are two types of cells within bone that are in delicate balance with each other during our lives; these are osteoclasts, which break down bone, and osteoblasts, which make bone. Bone is constantly being made and broken down, but bone strength should remain fairly constant.

Bones continue to strengthen from birth to about our late twenties, when they are at their strongest. From the age of about 35 onwards, we start to lose a small amount of bone density every year, which is normal. When the loss of density is greater than expected the condition is known either as osteopenia or osteoporosis, depending on how much bone density has been lost. Osteopenia is the term given to some reduction in the density of bones; osteoporosis is the term used when the bone density is very significantly reduced.

Osteoporosis

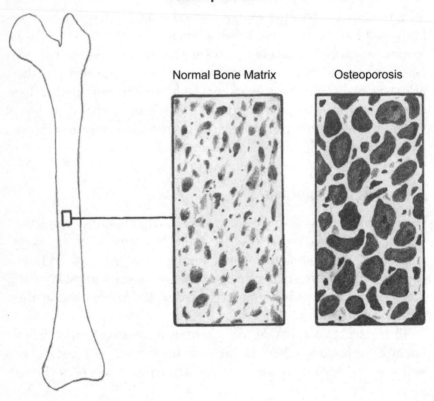

Normal Bone Matrix   Osteoporosis

Osteoporosis causes bones to break (fractures), and these are most commonly seen in the wrists, hips, ribs and spine.

As you get older your risk of getting a fracture dramatically increases. By the age of 80, one in three women will have experienced a hip fracture. The number of women with osteoporosis is growing rapidly, mostly due to women living much longer, less exercise and less calcium and vitamin D in our diet.

Risk Factors for Osteoporosis

Apart from getting older, other factors are associated with an increased risk of osteoporosis in women:

- Premature menopause, i.e. periods stopping permanently at the age of 40 or less
- Prolonged periods of time without periods – often seen with anorexia sufferers and athletes
- Steroid therapy – for asthma, rheumatoid arthritis and so on
- Past history of fracture
- Thyroid disease
- Coeliac disease
- Lifestyle risk factors – poor dietary intake of calcium and vitamin D, alcohol, smoking, physical inactivity and minimal exposure to sunlight

What to Look Out For

Osteoporosis has no signs or symptoms. Loss of bone density itself does not cause pain or other symptoms; it is the resulting fracture, or a deformity resulting from a fracture, that causes pain. These are most commonly seen in the wrist, spine and hip. Examples of what to look out for with osteoporosis include:

- Fragility fractures – these are fractures caused by a seemingly insignificant fall. Adults in general should not break a bone from a trip and fall from standing position.
- A deformity of the upper back caused by fractures in the back bone or vertebrae. This is also known as a dowager's hump.
- A loss of height of 2 cm to 16 cm
- Development of sharp, sudden back pain with associated height loss

Diagnosis

The best way to diagnose osteoporosis is dual energy x-ray absorptiometry (DEXA). This is a simple test done in the x-ray department which involves taking x-rays of the spine and hips. It is painless and very quick.

The DEXA test measures the bone mineral density (BMD) of the spine and both hips. A measurement is then done, called the T-score, which classifies the BMD into the following:

- A normal T-score is defined as 0 to -1.0.
- Osteopenia is defined as a T-score of -1.0 to -2.49, i.e. mild bone loss.
- Osteoporosis is defined as a T-score of lower than -2.5, i.e. moderate to severe bone loss.

A diagnosis is then usually made by your doctor based on the T-score from the DEXA scan. Most fractures occur in the T-score range of -1.5 to -2.49, so it is very important to treat these women to prevent them from getting fractures in the future.

What Can I Do?

In general, regardless of your DEXA result, there are certain lifestyle changes that you should make in the areas of diet, exercise and fall prevention:

Diet

Calcium and vitamin D are both essential for good bone health. Vitamin D is also necessary for the body to absorb calcium from food. Unfortunately, they are often lacking in women for several reasons:

- Low levels of calcium and vitamin D in the diet
- Poor skin exposure to sunlight
- Low oestrogen levels, such as with women after the menopause; this makes calcium absorption from food less efficient.

Dairy produce, leafy green vegetables and tinned fish, such as sardines and salmon, are all excellent sources of calcium. Vitamin D is not present in many foodstuffs but can be taken as a daily supplement. Exposure to ultraviolet rays from the sun for 20 minutes per day triggers the manufacture of vitamin D within the body.

A Guide to the Calcium Content of Foods
(Recommended daily intake is 800–1000 mg/day)

Food	Quantity	Calcium (Mg)
Milk – skimmed	100 ml	122
Milk – semi skimmed	100 ml	120
Milk – whole	100 ml	118
Soya milk	100 ml	89
Cheddar cheese	100 g	739
Low fat hard cheese	100 g	840
Low fat fruit yogurt	100 g	140
Sardines (in oil)	100 g	500
Curly kale (boiled)	100 g	150
Red kidney beans (canned)	100 g	71

(Continued)

(Continued)

Food	Quantity	Calcium (Mg)
Tahini	100 g	680
Tofu (steamed)	100 g	510
White bread	100 g	177
Wholemeal bread	100 g	106
Muesli (Swiss style)	100 g	110
Figs (dried)	100 g	250
Apricots (dried)	100 g	73

Source: adapted from information provided by the National Osteoporois Society, UK, available from www.nos.org.uk/Document.doc?id=395, accessed 07 January 2013.

It is recommended that if your periods have stopped you should try and consume 1,200 mg of calcium in your diet every day, and vitamin D supplements should be started if your level of vitamin D in your blood is not high enough. Your doctor can check this for you with a simple blood test. You will need 800 IU of vitamin D per day.

Exercise

Exercise is a very important part of the overall health picture for postmenopausal woman, as certain forms of exercise will stop bones from thinning. This exercise must be weight bearing, such as running, walking, skipping, dancing and so on. This will also maintain fitness levels, balance and co-ordination, which will help to reduce the risk of falling – a big consideration for older women. Balance exercises such as yoga or t'ai chi are also useful. Exercise that presents a risk of falling should be avoided.

Preventing Falls

Fall prevention is very important for older women. Simple measures such as regular eye testing, spotting possible hazards in the home, use of hip protectors by thin women, and identification of certain medical conditions seen in the elderly, such as postural hypotension (sudden drop in blood pressure on standing up quickly leading to dizziness), are all useful in reducing the risk of fractures. A hip protector is a form of girdle with reinforced padding on the hip areas which reduces the chances of a hip fracture if you fall while wearing it. Other measures that can be useful are bathtub bars to aid getting in and out of the bath, avoiding sedating medication and wearing well-fitting shoes.

Treatments for Osteoporosis

There are several drugs used to treat osteoporosis, and the choice depends on the overall DEXA result, the areas where bone loss is most marked, and your age and general health. The aim of treatment is always prevention of fracture by stopping further bone loss and increasing bone density. In practice, the agents used for both treatment and prevention are the same. The use of preventative treatments should be confined to patients at the highest risk of osteoporosis.

All the available treatments have some side effects but, in general, the benefits outweigh these side effects. Sometimes it is difficult for a patient to be expected to keep taking medication every day for a condition that does not cause them any symptoms, particularly if the medication has side effects. Regular DEXA measurements can assess what improvement in the bone density has been achieved, and this can help to convince the patient that treatment is worthwhile.

Bisphosphonates

This is probably one of the most well-known treatments. Bisphosphonates are a group of drugs which stop osteoclasts from doing their job of breaking down bone, so over time the bone density increases. Bisphosphonates are available as daily, weekly and monthly preparations.

Bisphosphonates are associated with side effects in the oesophagus or food pipe, mainly inflammation. This can be prevented by taking the medication with a large glass of water 30 minutes before eating first thing in the morning, and remaining upright for 30 minutes after taking it. The length of time that you will need to take this treatment is uncertain, but it can be up to ten years. We do know that the increases seen in your bone density while you are taking bisphosphonates remain for several years after you stop using it.

Denosumab

This is one of the more recent additions to the range of products available in the treatment of osteoporosis. It works by stopping osteoclasts from developing and, therefore, slows bone breakdown. It is given as an injection under the skin every six months and has been shown to reduce the numbers of fractures at both the hip and spine.

Hormone Replacement Therapy (HRT)

This was previously used widely for osteoporosis in women who had reached the menopause. Nowadays it is used less frequently, although it can be more commonly used in one particular type of patient, i.e. if you have recently started to develop menopausal symptoms and you have been found to have some reduced bone density on DEXA scan. This is also known as osteopenia, which is associated with a low risk of fracture. There is a small fracture reduction seen with HRT, which is lost after discontinuing the therapy. It is generally accepted that to maintain any gain in bone density, another medication such as a bisphosphanate then needs to be used.

What HRT does is provide us with another treatment option which will keep your bones healthy during your fifties while your menopausal symptoms may be troublesome, allowing medications such as bisphosphonates to be reserved for later decades when fracture risk is much greater. The rule of prescribing HRT – 'as little as possible for as short a time as possible' – holds true for the treatment of osteopenia and osteoporosis, in view of the possible slight increase in breast cancer incidence in women using HRT for prolonged periods over five years.

Selective Oestrogen Receptor Modulators (SERMs)

SERMs have been shown to reduce the risk of fractures of the spine. They are administered as a daily tablet. SERMs only behave like oestrogen in bone, and studies have shown a reduction in breast cancer risk with their use. Unfortunately, this treatment can cause hot flushes as a side effect.

Strontium Ranelate

Strontium ranelate is a drug which reduces fractures in both the hip and spine. It acts by preventing bone breakdown and stimulating bone formation. It is taken in granule form daily and has few side effects.

Parathyroid Hormone

This is a pharmaceutical form of parathyroid hormone (PTH). It is prescribed by consultants only and is indicated for women at high risk of fracture. It stimulates new bone formation and is administered daily by the patient by self-injection for 24 months.

Teriparatide

This is an artificial form of PTH which acts by building bone and reduces fracture risk. It is only prescribed by a consultant and is administered by the patient by self-injection daily for 24 months. It can also help with pain from vertebral fractures.

Conclusions

Osteoporosis is extremely common and, unfortunately, increasing due to our ageing population. The problem with osteoporosis is not just the fractures themselves; bone fractures can prevent older women who are otherwise well from living independently. For elderly women over 65 years of age, 25 per cent of them will die within one year of a hip fracture, due to other illnesses resulting from the fracture, such as blood clots or pneumonia due to reduced mobility.

We have no national screening programme for osteoporosis in Ireland like the cervical smear or mammogram programmes which are already available. This may have to change as osteoporosis becomes more of a health problem. Prevention is hugely important in managing this disease, as the cost of this disease is huge both to the patient and to the health care system.

Lifestyle changes can help prevent or treat osteoporosis and should be discussed with all newly-postmenopausal women. For the moment, DEXA scans should be offered to all women around the time of the menopause who are thought to be at risk of developing osteoporosis, or earlier if obvious risk factors are present.

Key Points

- Osteoporosis affects one in three women over 50 years of age.
- Osteoporosis causes no symptoms, until you break a bone.

- Risk factors include a family history of osteoporosis, smoking, a low BMI, early menopause, steroid use and coeliac disease.
- A variety of treatments are available, depending on your age and results of your DEXA bone density scan.
- Sufficient calcium and vitamin D in your diet, as well as weight-bearing exercises are important to help treat osteoporosis.

12

Gastrointestinal Problems

Several illnesses of the gastrointestinal tract are dealt with in this chapter. Most of the conditions discussed are not serious, but cause a lot of distress and discomfort for women. Dietary changes are key to treating all of them.

Irritable Bowel Syndrome (IBS)

IBS is an extremely common condition of the large bowel, estimated to affect up to 20 per cent of the population at some stage in their lives. It mostly starts in younger people in their twenties and thirties, and women are more affected by IBS than men.

Signs and Symptoms of IBS

The main symptoms of IBS include abdominal cramping, pain, bloating, diarrhoea and constipation. For some, the symptoms come and go; for others they are constant. In the case of diarrhoea, the amount of time that waste material spends in the large colon is too short. Not enough water is reabsorbed by the colon back into the body, leading to watery diarrhoea. In the case of constipation, the time spent in the colon is too long, allowing for excessive amounts of water reabsorption, thus leaving hard waste material for excretion. Bloating is caused by overproduction of gas, because the waste is lingering for too long in the colon. IBS can also cause too much mucus production, which can be seen coating the bowel motion.

IBS never causes weight loss, bleeding or severe pain, and this is how it is differentiated from more serious but much less common bowel conditions such as Crohn's disease and ulcerative colitis.

Gastrointestinal Tract

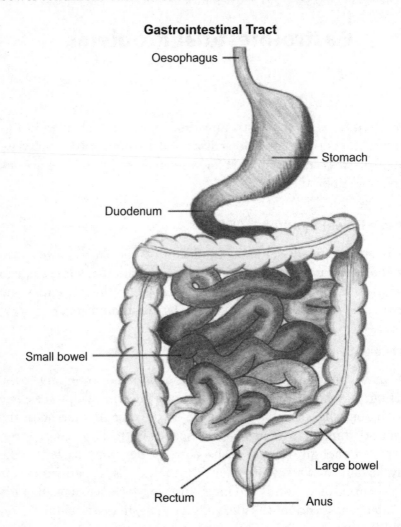

Causes of IBS

It is not fully understood what causes IBS but some evidence shows that it may be due to a chemical in the body called serotonin, which controls the muscle of the bowel. It is possible that in cases of IBS there is a change in the sensitivity to serotonin which leads to over- or underactivity in the bowel. IBS is also seen following infection of the bowel, and it can also occur in association with stress and anxiety, suggesting that there is a psychological element to this physical condition.

How to Diagnose IBS

In order to be diagnosed with IBS, you need to have the following indications:

- Certain symptoms must be present, including bloating, constipation, an uncontrollable urge to pass a bowel motion and the presence of mucus.
- These symptoms must be present for twelve weeks out of the previous twelve months; the weeks do not need to be consecutive.
- Your abdominal pain improves after a bowel motion.
- When an episode of IBS starts, the pattern and appearance of the bowel motion changes.

IBS can be diagnosed mainly from your description of symptoms. Physical examination is normal, and blood tests to check for coeliac disease and anaemia should also be done. A colonoscopy should be considered for those aged over 40 with a new onset of symptoms.

How to Treat IBS

IBS is treated by controlling symptoms in a lot of cases. It is important to remember that most women with IBS will have mild symptoms and will manage their condition very well, remaining comfortable on the whole. However, if your symptoms are proving difficult to control, the following is a list of treatment options:

Diet

Although diet undoubtedly plays a significant role in both the cause and control of symptoms, everyone is, unfortunately, different, and what some people find tolerable in their diet others will not. It is very helpful to keep a food diary for a few days to help try and identify foods which may trigger your symptoms. That way you can eliminate foods in a systematic way as part of your treatment plan.

Changing your fibre content can help with your symptoms. There are two kinds of fibre – insoluble and soluble. Examples of each include:

- Insoluble – wholegrain bread, brans, cereals, nuts and seeds
- Soluble – oats, rye, fruits like apple and banana, barley, carrots and potatoes

If diarrhoea is a predominant feature, reducing your insoluble fibre intake can help. If constipation is a symptom, increasing the soluble fibre content in your diet, as well as including 2 litres of water daily, may improve constipation.

General eating tips for IBS sufferers include:

- Reduce alcohol and fizzy drink intake.
- Eat food slowly.
- Consume a maximum of three cups of coffee/tea per day.
- Drink eight glasses of non-caffeinated drinks per day.
- Limit fresh fruit to three portions per day.
- Keep meals small and frequent, with no long gaps between meals.

- Eliminate or at least reduce wheat, rye, barley, milk products, chocolate and alcohol.

Exercise

Regular exercise will improve IBS symptoms. This may be due to a release of natural relaxants following exercise, or it may be the help that exercise gives by stimulating bowel muscle. Vigorous exercise for at least 30 minutes, three to five times a week may be required.

Probiotics

Although scientific research has yet to prove that probiotics help with IBS symptoms, some patients do report an improvement. These can be taken as a course of tablets which are available from pharmacies and health food shops.

Reducing Stress

The majority of patients with persistent IBS admit that stress plays a part in their control of symptoms. Techniques to reduce stress include meditation, hypnotherapy, yoga and regular exercise. If simple measures such as these are not helping, a different approach such as cognitive behavioural therapy (CBT) may be helpful. This is a form of short-term therapy which asserts that the way you think determines to some extent the way you feel. Therefore, if you can learn new ways of thinking about IBS and your symptoms, you will get good relief from your symptoms. This can be a highly successful treatment option.

Antispasmodics

These medications are usually available over the counter. They work by reducing muscle spasm or cramp in the bowel muscle in response to eating. They are usually taken before eating. Common antispasmodics include mebeverine (Colofac) and peppermint oil (Colpermin).

Antidiarrhoeal Medication

In patients for whom diarrhoea is a problem, a simple antidiarrhoeal, such as loperamide (Lomotil) can help.

Laxatives

For patients with constipation, a laxative such as macrogol (Movicol) can be helpful. The lowest dosage should be started and increased gradually until a soft bowel motion is achieved every day.

Antidepressants

There are two main types of antidepressants used in IBS: tricyclic antidepressants (TCAs) and selective serotonin re-uptake inhibitors (SSRIs). These work by relaxing the muscles in the colon which are causing pain through excessive spasm.

Coeliac Disease

Coeliac disease is a surprisingly common condition in Ireland, with up to one in one hundred people affected. It is almost certainly under-diagnosed, in other words a lot of people have coeliac disease in a mild form but are not aware of it. It has significant implications for your health in the long term so it is important to know about how it can affect you, and you should ask to be tested for it if you have some of the symptoms.

Causes of Coeliac Disease

The majority of the food that we absorb within the gut is absorbed in the small intestine, which is a large tube connecting the stomach to the colon. The nutrients from food are absorbed by millions of tiny finger-like projections called villi. In coeliac disease, gluten, which is a type of protein, causes an allergic reaction in the villi, destroying them. This in turn leads to a lack of absorption of fat, protein and sugars, as well as vitamins and minerals. This poor absorption causes symptoms such as diarrhoea, pain, bloating and excessive gas, as well as signs such as weight loss and anaemia.

Coeliac disease can become apparent in babies, in children and in adults. Babies typically develop diarrhoea, bloating, smelly bowel motions (seen when fat is not being properly absorbed), irritability and failure to grow and thrive. This occurs after cereal-based foods have been introduced in the first year.

Signs and Symptoms of Coeliac Disease

In young children, coeliac disease typically presents as diarrhoea, fatty bowel motions, excessive gas, poor growth and weight loss. In adults, symptoms such as diarrhoea, fatty bowel motions, pain and excessive gas can be seen. However, in some adults the only symptoms are mild abdominal discomfort or iron-deficiency anaemia. In fact, 15 per cent of all adult cases of coeliac disease are detected on blood test only; the patients themselves have no symptoms.

In 10 per cent of cases an itchy rash is seen with coeliac disease, called dermatitis herpetiformis, which can occur on the legs, buttocks, body and scalp. Painful recurrent mouth ulcers are also seen in association with coeliac disease. Not surprisingly, coeliac disease is more commonly seen in patients with other autoimmune diseases, such as rheumatoid arthritis and lupus. Long-term complications of coeliac disease in adults include osteoporosis, anaemia and bowel cancer.

Diagnosis of Coeliac Disease

Coeliac disease is confirmed by a biopsy of the small intestine, done at the time of an oesophago-gastro-duodenoscopy (OGD). This is an outpatient procedure and involves a flexible camera being swallowed by the patient in order to inspect the upper gastrointestinal area. A tiny piece of the small bowel is taken at the time of the procedure and examined microscopically for the changes typically seen with coeliac disease. The patient should have been on a gluten-containing diet for two weeks prior to the test.

Blood tests are also available which are very good at detecting coeliac disease. If these tests are abnormal there is a 95 per cent chance that the patient will have coeliac disease.

It has been suggested that the following groups should have blood tests to check for coeliac disease:

* Children with poor growth
* Patients with diarrhoea for more than three weeks with associated weight loss
* Patients with recurrent mouth ulcers
* First degree relatives of people with coeliac disease, i.e. parents and siblings
* Patients with excessive gas and bloating
* Patients with unexplained iron deficiency
* Patients with rashes suggestive of dermatitis herpetiformis
* Women with other illnesses, such as diabetes, rheumatoid arthritis, autoimmune thyroid diseases and lupus

Treatment of Coeliac Disease

Treatment of coeliac disease involves the complete exclusion of gluten from the diet as soon as the diagnosis is made. This includes products containing wheat, barley, bulgur, durum wheat, semolina and spelt. Symptoms improve quickly in adults, usually within a few weeks. However, the intestinal tract can take much longer to completely heal. When a gluten-free diet has been introduced in children, improved growth usually follows. Consultation with a dietician can help you plan a healthy gluten-free diet.

Constipation

Constipation is defined as less than three bowel motions per week. Severe constipation is defined as less than one bowel motion per week. It can also be defined as excessive straining at the time of defecation (passing a bowel motion), or passing small hard pellets of stool.

It is twice as common in women as men, and is more common in older women but is seen in all age groups. Forty per cent of pregnant women will experience constipation during their pregnancy.

It can affect people for short, limited periods of times, and resolve without treatment. However, it can also be a chronic condition which can cause problems on an ongoing basis if not addressed.

Signs and Symptoms of Constipation

As you would expect, one of the main symptoms of constipation is a change in the appearance of your stool. It is usually hard and lumpy, and can be unusually large or unusually small. Constipation can be associated with bloating, cramps and excessive wind. It can also be associated with pain in the anal area, caused by the presence of haemorrhoids or piles (see below). The hard stool can cause the skin to split at the edge of the anus, causing an anal fissure. The presence of a fissure can complicate constipation, as often voluntary constipation occurs. The natural urge to pass a bowel motion occurs, but it is suppressed as pain is anticipated when a bowel motion is passed.

Causes of Constipation

The vast majority of cases of constipation are not due to any specific cause or condition. However, there are some factors which are more likely to bring about constipation:

- Dehydration
- Sedentary lifestyle
- Low dietary intake of fibre
- A change in routine or diet
- Ignoring the urge to defecate
- Inadequate privacy when going to the toilet
- Depression
- Being overweight or underweight
- Pregnancy – during pregnancy a hormone called progesterone is produced in large amounts. This is a muscle relaxant, and allows the colon muscles to relax excessively, leading to a slower time for food to pass through the colon.
- Prescribed medications – some medications can cause constipation, such as antidepressants, calcium supplements, iron supplements, antacids, anti-epileptics, pain medication containing codeine, and diuretics for elevated blood pressure. Your doctor should be able to change your medication to improve the constipation.
- In unusual cases, an underlying medical condition is the cause of constipation, including hypothyroidism, multiple sclerosis and colon cancer.

Diagnosis of Constipation

The diagnosis of constipation is mostly done through a discussion with your doctor, during which they will ask a series of questions relating to your symptoms, lifestyle, dietary habits and toilet habits. Remember, this problem is most likely going to be sorted out by changing your behaviours, so the more information you can give your doctor the better. Don't feel embarrassed about discussing this – your doctor won't be.

In some cases where the constipation has suddenly started, and there are associated worrying symptoms, such as unexplained weight loss, a colonoscopy should be performed. This is where the bowel is closely examined under anaesthetic using a camera inserted through the rectum. Blood tests to rule out hypothyroidism and anaemia could also be considered, depending on the overall picture given by the patient. In particular, if the patient is not responding within a few weeks with simple measures, further investigations should be started.

Treatments for Constipation

The aim of treating constipation is to achieve a bowel motion of normal consistency every two to three days. Simple measures should be introduced at the start which may prevent having to use laxatives at all. These include:

- Learning what a high fibre diet is, as this is the bare minimum required to correct constipation. A high fibre diet should include at least five portions of fruit and vegetables per day, wholegrain pasta, rice and bread, nuts, seed and oats.
- Never ignoring the urge to defecate, and ensuring that privacy and time is allowed to enable this to happen
- Increasing water intake to eight glasses of water each day
- Exercising for 20 minutes daily
- Introducing wheat bran or linseed into the diet to try and increase the size of the bowel motion

If these measures are not successful, then a laxative should be introduced. Remember each treatment introduced should be given a few weeks to work, as bowel habits will not change overnight.

Laxatives

These are used to treat constipation when the simple measures mentioned above have not been successful. Macrogol (Movicol) works by increasing the volume of water in the bowel, thus preventing the bowel motion for drying out and becoming hard, as well as stimulating the bowel. It is used in increasing doses until the desired result has been achieved. An effect is usually seen within three days of starting a laxative, and fluid intake should be increased while taking it. Other examples of laxatives include bulk-forming laxatives (e.g. psyllium husks), which are high in fibre and therefore increase the size of the bowel motion, and stool softeners (e.g. Dulcolax), which help to lubricate the stool and make defecation less painful.

Stimulant Laxatives

These work by artificially stimulating the bowel to contract and, therefore, produce a bowel motion. They are relatively fast acting – usually within 6 to 12 hours. Some stimulant laxatives, in particular those containing senna, are readily available over the counter, but they should be used with caution. Senna is a naturally-occurring substance, which is commonly used because of its laxative properties. Long-term use of stimulant laxatives has been associated with poor colon muscle function, leading to further constipation.

Haemorrhoids

Haemorrhoids, also known as piles, are swollen, painful veins at the anus or just inside the anus in the rectum. They are most commonly caused by excessive straining when passing a bowel motion, and are closely linked to constipation. They are also very commonly seen in pregnancy and immediately after childbirth.

Symptoms of Haemorrhoids

The symptoms of haemorrhoids include:

- Pain in the anal area during or after defecation
- A soft swelling felt at the anus
- Anal itching
- Bright red blood passed from the anus, often seen on wiping the area after a bowel motion and in the toilet bowl; the blood is not mixed in with the stool.

Diagnosis of Haemorrhoids

Your doctor will be able to diagnose haemorrhoids by a simple examination. Sometimes if the haemorrhoids are not immediately obvious externally a test called a sigmoidoscopy can be performed to examine the rectum internally.

Treatments for Haemorrhoids

- Simple measures such as changing your diet to include a higher insoluble fibre content will help food to pass through your colon quicker. Sources of insoluble fibre are fruits and vegetables, wholegrain cereals and breads. Water intake should be increased.
- When cleaning your bottom, you could use baby wipes which are gentler on the skin, and do not vigorously rub the area.
- Over the counter creams (e.g. Anusol) will help with symptoms, but should not be used for long periods.
- Local anaesthetic creams can be used in the short term to relieve pain.
- Stool softeners may be needed to reduce the pain associated with a bowel motion while the haemorrhoids are painful.

- Steroid creams and suppositories will help to shrink the haemorrhoids but should not be used for more than one week at a time.
- Banding is a procedure whereby a tight band is applied to the external haemorrhoid, which shuts of its blood supply. The haemorrhoid shrinks and disappears some time later.
- Sclerotic injections can be used to treat haemorrhoids. These are given under local anaesthetic and a chemical agent is injected into the haemorrhoids, causing them to shrink significantly.
- Surgical removal of haemorrhoids is sometimes necessary.

The blood inside haemorrhoids can clot, causing the haemorrhoid to swell significantly and become extremely painful in a short period of time. In these circumstances, the clot may need to be removed from inside the haemorrhoid under local anaesthetic.

Key Points

- Irritable bowel syndrome (IBS) causes bloating, pain and a change in bowel habit, and can usually be controlled by diet changes.
- Coeliac disease is common in Irish women, but in some women the symptoms are mild and the diagnosis is often not made.
- Coeliac disease can cause anaemia and osteoporosis as well as abdominal symptoms.
- Constipation can usually be greatly improved with diet changes, increased water intake and exercise; however, in some cases laxatives are required.
- Haemorrhoids are usually caused by constipation, and cause bleeding, pain and itching around the anus.

13

Menopause

The word menopause comes from the Greek words *pausis* (stopping) and *men* (monthly). This literally means that when your periods have stopped you are menopausal. However, menopausal symptoms can begin long before your periods stop. This is called the perimenopause. Once your periods have stopped for twelve months or longer this is called the postmenopausal period. It is now accepted that the menopause is a series of hormonal changes over time, during which women's experiences can differ enormously.

When we are born we have a certain number of unripened eggs or follicles in the ovaries, which, over our reproductive lives, are used up during ovulation each month. From a girl's first menstrual cycle in her early teens, a certain number of follicles are 'recruited' each month. The strongest or dominant follicle is the one which finally releases the ovum or egg at ovulation.

Eventually around midlife most of the follicles are used up, and hormone production from the ovaries starts to fall. It is the falling hormone levels that cause menopausal symptoms which can be so problematic. In Irish women, the average age at which periods stop is 50, but this can be earlier in smokers or women with chronic disease.

However, long before periods stop completely, the dropping hormone levels can cause many symptoms. We call this the perimenopause, or climacteric.

A surgical menopause happens when both ovaries are surgically removed. This creates an instant menopause, as the source of all oestrogen is suddenly removed. Menopausal symptoms in these women can be quite severe, as there is no gentle introduction to the menopause with slowly reducing oestrogen levels as with a natural menopause.

A hysterectomy, on the other hand, simply stops periods, as only the womb has been removed; the menopause will occur naturally because the ovaries have been left in place. However, any pelvic surgery, including hysterectomy, is associated with a slightly younger age for the onset of menopause. Chemotherapy and radiotherapy can also irreversibly damage the ovaries, bringing about the menopause.

Signs and Symptoms

About 70 per cent of women will experience menopausal symptoms, but only 10 per cent will ask for help from their doctor. This is because most women will find their symptoms manageable. Nevertheless, some women will experience symptoms which are sufficiently severe to significantly affect their quality of life. Symptoms can differ quite a lot depending on where you are in relation to the menopause process.

Perimenopause symptoms include:

- Changes in your periods, including a shorter cycle, longer cycle, heavier bleed, etc.
- Worsening premenstrual symptoms
- Mood swings
- Irritability
- Forgetfulness
- Insomnia
- Premenstrual night sweats

- Poor concentration
- Exhaustion
- Poor libido

Postmenopausal symptoms can include:

- Periods stopping
- Hot flushes
- Night sweats
- Vaginal dryness
- Thinning of hair
- Urinary problems – frequency, burning, stress incontinence, etc.
- Prolapse

How Do I Know if I Am Becoming Menopausal?

One of the first signs of the menopause is a change in your menstrual cycle. This can be the length of your cycle changing – usually shortening by seven days or more. In other words, if your cycle is normally 31 days, you may find that your cycle is now 24 days. The period itself may become longer or heavier, or both. Symptoms of premenstrual syndrome (PMS) can appear for the first time, or become much worse. Some women may continue to have a regular cycle, but may experience symptoms like exhaustion and mood swings. These can be more obvious in the seven to ten days leading up to your period.

This stage in the menopause process often causes great confusion, as women assume or are told by their doctors that 'you can't be menopausal; you are still having periods'. From a clinical point of view, the diagnosis lies in listening to the woman; her description of her symptoms will confirm the fact that this is the start of perimenopause. A blood test to check the level of follicle-stimulating hormone (FSH) can often be done at this time. FSH is a hormone produced in the pituitary gland in the brain. As oestrogen levels start to fall this hormone starts to rise, and an FSH reading over 30 on two separate occasions three months apart diagnoses menopause. However, in the perimenopausal phase the FSH level can vary from being high to being normal. This variation in FSH level can vary from hour to hour and, therefore, it is very difficult to 'catch' the FSH at a high level. Unfortunately, what often happens is that your doctor will interpret a normal FSH result as meaning that you are definitely not menopausal. This can lead to a lot of confusion and upset. A newer test, anti-Müllerian hormone (AMH), can be useful in diagnosing the menopause. AMH is low at the time of menopause.

Treatments Available

The most important thing to do is to talk to your doctor about your symptoms. If you don't feel he/she will be the right person for you to discuss this with, find another doctor! This is not a mystery illness – there are lots of competent doctors who are able to diagnose and treat the menopause appropriately.

Sometimes just putting a name to what is causing your symptoms is such a relief that no drug treatment is necessary. Most women are not looking for medication. Once they understand what is happening to them, and are given lots of information about why this is happening, how long it will last, and what to expect over the next few years, most women are happy just to continue on as they are without medical intervention. Some simple advice about lifestyle measures can also make an enormous difference.

What You Can Do

There are several things you can do when you reach the menopause to help ease your symptoms:

Dietary Changes

There are lots of changes you can make to your diet to try to improve your general wellbeing. Some of them you will undoubtedly have seen before in relation to general weight loss, but they are particularly important at the menopause when energy levels are low, weight gain can be a problem and certain foods will improve or worsen menopausal symptoms.

The following are some guidelines on how to eat better during the menopause:

- Avoid hot, spicy foods, particularly around your prime hot flush time of the day.
- Change to decaffeinated drinks, and try having an iced version instead of a hot drink.
- Reduce your intake of high fat, high sugar foods – they reduce your energy levels and leave you sluggish.
- Have five portions of fruit and vegetables every day.
- Eat smaller meals but more frequently, up to six very small meals per day; big meals make you hotter.
- Have a well-balanced breakfast – it will stabilise your sugar levels and make it less likely that you snack during the day.
- Increase the amount of fibre in your diet – brown bread, bran and cereals; fibre keeps you feeling fuller for longer.
- Increase your water intake.
- Try to introduce foods rich in folic acid, vitamin B12, selenium, calcium and omega 3 fatty acids, as they are all useful for energy and mood.
- Avoid alcohol – it causes hot flushes and depresses your mood.
- In some cases, the introduction of phytoestrogen-rich foods (see alternative therapies below) may help to alleviate some symptoms of the menopause.

Exercise

Exercise for the menopausal woman is very important for lots of reasons. It helps you to sleep better, aids weight loss, combats stress and tension, and generally improves the quality of life of women at this potentially difficult time. Fast walking or cardiovascular exercise tailored to your specific abilities is the most suitable form of exercise. More gentle forms of exercise, such as yoga, which teach controlled breathing techniques can be very useful in coping with such symptoms as flushes and sweats.

Stop Smoking

Yet another reason to stop! Smokers experience an earlier menopause, and their symptoms tend to be more severe than for non-smokers.

Non-hormonal Menopausal Treatments

These are a group of various drugs used for other medical conditions which have also been noted to reduce menopausal symptoms. They tend to be reserved for women whose symptoms are extremely severe but who cannot use oestrogen-containing HRT in any circumstances, such as women with breast cancer. The side effects of these medications can be quite noticeable, so they would not be suitable for everyone.

Clonidine

This is a medication used in the control of high blood pressure and also for migraine control. Its effect is to reduce the intensity of hot flushes, but its success is limited. The dose is usually 50 to 75 mg twice daily, and side effects can include dry mouth, dizziness and insomnia. It is not prescribed very often nowadays.

Antidepressants

A particular type of antidepressant medication called selective serotonin re-uptake inhibitors (SSRIs) and serotonin-noradrenaline re-uptake inhibitors (SNRIs) can help to reduce the quantity of hot flushes. They work in the brain near the heat control centre. Venlafaxine (Effexor), fluoxetine (Prozac) and paroxetine (Seroxat) have all been shown to work. Venlafaxine can reduce flushes by up to 50 per cent.

Progestogens

These are synthetic forms of progesterone, a hormone produced by our ovaries. When these are given in high doses they can relieve hot flushes, but side effects include bloating and fluid retention, which women cannot always tolerate.

Alternative Therapies

Every woman would like a safe, natural way of combating menopausal symptoms. Unfortunately, there is very little scientific evidence that alternative therapies are effective in relieving menopausal symptoms. There is little regulation over herbal products and food supplements, in direct contrast with the pharmaceutical industry. The actual strength of the naturally-occurring substances is largely unknown; the amount of active substance in each product is unregulated; and there may be active substances in the product which are unknown.

When a pharmaceutical drug has been discovered, it first has to undergo rigorous testing in the laboratory, initially on animals and then in human trials for many years before being released to the market. Why should naturally-occurring substances be any different? There are ongoing studies to look at both herbal products and food supplements to see if they have some role to play in the relief of symptoms like hot flushes. Nevertheless, it has yet to be established if they are completely safe to take, and they certainly cannot be recommended for patients on specific medications, such as blood-thinning drugs, blood pressure medication or antidepressants, or for patients with a history of liver disease or with a history of a hormone-related cancer, such as breast or endometrial cancer. Remember 'natural' is not always 'safe'. Check with your doctor before starting an alternative therapy to make sure it is safe for you. Below are some alternative therapies which may be worth trying.

Phytoestrogens

In certain suitable patients introducing foods rich in oestrogen – like substances such as phytoestrogens – can improve symptoms, although this has yet to be shown scientifically. The interest in phytoestrogens came from studying Japanese women who, in general, have very few menopausal symptoms. It is thought that the high content of soy in their diet may contribute to this, as soy has a very high phytoestrogen content. However, such large changes to a Western diet are difficult to achieve, and the levels of phytoestrogens required to relieve menopausal symptoms may prove too difficult. Foods rich in phytoestrogens include soy products, flaxseed or linseed, all kinds of beans, seeds and red clover.

Herbal Treatments

These include black cohosh, agnus castus and ginkgo biloba. Although not proven to be effective in some studies, these are still powerful, naturally-occurring substances which have significant effects on the body. They should only be used in certain patients and with the approval of your doctor beforehand.

Complementary Therapies

These include homeopathy, reflexology, aromatherapy, massage and acupuncture. These treatments have not been shown to have a specific effect on menopausal symptoms. Complementary therapies have a holistic approach and, therefore, aim to improve a woman's wellbeing in general. Some women find that they do benefit from using these therapies, and they would appear to be safe when carried out by a qualified practitioner.

Hormone Replacement Therapy (HRT)

The advantages and disadvantages of HRT have been debated for decades. There is undoubtedly a role for HRT in some patients, but the idea that it is suitable for all and to be recommended for all women is long gone. The main reasons for using HRT are primarily the control of menopausal symptoms and, to a lesser extent, the treatment of osteoporosis in women of menopausal age. The general rule when using HRT is as follows: 'Use as little as possible for the shortest time possible.'

Types of HRT

Depending on your situation, different types or regimens of HRT are recommended:

- If you still have a womb, a combination of oestrogen and progestogen is needed. The daily dose of oestrogen relieves the menopausal symptoms, whereas the progestogen balances the oestrogen and prevents the lining of the womb from thickening up excessively. Long-term use of oestrogen without progestogen can lead to cancer of the lining of the womb (endometrium).

- Women who are still having periods, or who have had a period in the last year, require a combination of oestrogen for 28 days and progestogen for 14 days, which allows them to have a monthly bleed. This is known as sequential HRT.
- Women who have not had a period for a year or more require a combination of both oestrogen and progestogen daily for 28 days in a lower dosage, which allows them to be bleed free. This is known as continuous combined HRT.
- Women who have had a hysterectomy require only oestrogen as their hormone replacement.

Ways of Taking HRT

There are several ways of taking HRT, although our options in Ireland are slightly more limited than in the UK or USA. These include:

Oral Form

Both oestrogen and progestogen come in tablet form. They can be taken individually or combined in a single tablet.

Patch

Patches can be in oestrogen-only form for women who have had hysterectomies, or in combination with progestogen. They can be given as a weekly or a twice-weekly dose, depending on the particular brand.

Vaginal

The only vaginal form of hormone replacement is that of local oestrogen. This is not absorbed into the bloodstream and, therefore, is not effective in relieving menopausal symptoms. It is very useful in relieving local vaginal and urethral symptoms, such as dryness, soreness and urinary frequency and urgency seen in postmenopausal women. It can be used safely in almost all women, as its effect is localised in the vagina.

Intrauterine System (IUS)

An IUS such as the Mirena coil delivers a daily dose of progestogen directly into the womb via a slow-release system which lasts for five years. This is sufficient progestogen to balance oestrogen given in any other form and, therefore, makes delivery of HRT easier.

How Quickly Does it Work?

HRT works very quickly to relieve menopausal symptoms, and you should feel a significant improvement within ten days of starting treatment.

When Do You Stop?

While you are on HRT, the natural process of the menopause is continuing on. In other words, HRT disguises the menopause; it does not postpone it. For most women HRT is so successful at disguising their symptoms of menopause that they have to stop it in order to find out if they are still going through the menopause. For this reason it is advisable to stop every year to assess whether you have any remaining symptoms. When stopping HRT you should wean off it slowly over a period of about eight weeks, as this reduces the risk of getting 'rebound' symptoms. If you have been started on HRT in your forties for early or premature menopause you should continue to take it until you reach the age of 50.

Among those women who are starting it after the age of 50, there is often a big worry that they will end up taking it for long periods of time. The opposite is true. The average length of time that women use HRT is approximately eighteen months. This is usually because you become naturally curious as to what stage you are at in terms of the menopause process, and the temptation to come off it in order to find out is great. In a lot of cases the HRT never gets restarted, as women find that their remaining symptoms are manageable without HRT. Only a very small percentage of women will find their menopausal symptoms are adversely affecting their quality of life over a very prolonged period of time, and for those women long-term use of HRT can be an option. For everyone else, their HRT use comes to a natural end after a surprisingly short time.

Long-term Health Benefits of HRT

The long-term benefits of HRT include potential protection against cardiovascular disease and proven protection against osteoporosis. Some studies have shown mixed results with regard to the effect of HRT on the cardiovascular system, and this has caused confusion as to whether there is a risk of cardiovascular disease or a protective effect by using it. It seems that both may be true. Some large-scale American studies showed a slight increase in stroke and heart attack during the first year of use, but the average age of the women in these studies was 67. The significance of this is that women in this age group are not the target age group for HRT use. It would appear from looking at women between the ages of 45 and 55 who have used HRT in the past that there is a protective effect on the heart and blood vessels with HRT use, and that this age is the 'window of opportunity' in which to use HRT in order to protect the cardiovascular system later in life.

Bone Protection

HRT use has long been known to have a protective effect against osteoporosis. Generally speaking, different drug therapies may be recommended for women depending on the severity of the osteoporosis and on their age. HRT is ideal for women who are between the ages of 45 and 55 and who have been shown to have osteopenia or mild bone density loss, but who also need HRT to control their menopausal symptoms. If you are not experiencing menopausal symptoms, HRT is not necessarily appropriate to treat osteopenia or osteoporosis.

Short-term Side Effects of HRT

This refers to side effects that you might experience within the first few weeks or months after starting HRT. These are usually minor and will disappear if you persevere. They include irregular bleeding, headache, nausea and water retention. Occasionally, in some women they can be more severe, so it is always very important to let your doctor know if you are experiencing any side effects within the first few weeks of starting HRT. They will probably be able to reassure you that what you are experiencing is normal.

Long-term Health Worries with HRT

I think most women have heard something over the last decade about the concern regarding HRT use and an increase in the risk of developing breast cancer. Luckily this valuable information has come to light and allows us to inform patients accurately about the risks of HRT use. It has also helped to clarify the ideal length of time that patients should stay on HRT, and prevents patients from being left on it unnecessarily for long periods of time. The concept of taking as little HRT as possible to relieve symptoms and to stay on it for as short a time as possible is now universally accepted, and this is in no small part due to the large studies conducted which have uncovered the information regarding the breast cancer risk.

However, this information must be put in perspective. The international media did women in general no favours when they decided to pick up the 'HRT and breast cancer' story and publicise it as they did. What has happened now is that many women whose lives would be greatly improved by using HRT for a short period of time without any increased risk of breast cancer are not being prescribed it. Indeed, they themselves have formed an opinion that HRT is dangerous, based on media reports.

The Facts about HRT

- HRT does not increase a woman's risk of breast cancer unless it is taken for more than five to seven years, after which time a slight increase in breast cancer is seen. For women taking oestrogen only, i.e. women who have had a hysterectomy, no increase in risk is seen.
- For women between the ages of 50 to 70, breast cancer affects 45 per 1,000.
- If HRT is taken for more than five years, this increases to 47 per 1,000.
- If HRT is taken for more than ten years, this increases to 51 per 1,000.
- If HRT is taken for more than fifteen years, this increases to 57 per 1,000.

Source: the above information is based on research conducted by a Collaborative Group on Hormonal Factors in Breast Cancer, 1997, 'Breast Cancer and HRT: Collaborative Reanalysis of Data from 51 Epidemiological Studies of 52,705 Women with Breast Cancer and 108,411 Women without Breast Cancer', *The Lancet*, Vol. 350, Issue 9,089, pp. 1,484.

For women starting HRT for an early menopause who are between the ages of 40 and 45, and women who are experiencing a premature menopause (under the age of 40), there is no additional risk of breast cancer. This increased breast cancer risk is only seen in women aged over 50 using HRT for longer than five years. The increased risk is gone within five years of stopping HRT.

It should also be pointed out that several other risk factors for breast cancer pose a far greater risk than HRT, as the following chart highlights:

Number of Women Developing Breast Cancer Over Next Five Years

	(Per 1,000 women)
No HRT	15
Oestrogen-only HRT	11
Oestrogen/progestogen HRT	19
More than 2 units alcohol/day	23–30
BMI over 35	30

Source: adapted from a Women's Health Initiative trial, which studied 160,000 postmenopausal women over 15 years in the US.

As you can see, there is a reduction in the number of breast cancer cases in women using oestrogen-only HRT, a small increase in the combined HRT group, and a significantly larger increase in obese women and women who consume more than 2 units of alcohol per day.

Increased Risk of Blood Clotting with HRT

Tablet forms of HRT cause a slight increase in the risk of blood clots:

- The risk of a woman who is not on HRT getting a blood clot is 1 in 1,000 per year.
- The risk of a woman who is on HRT (tablet only) getting a blood clot is 2.5 in 1,000 per year.

It is usually advised that if a woman has had a clot in the past she should not use HRT, unless under the guidance of a specialist. If there is a family history of blood clotting or thrombosis, a blood test can be done for the woman to determine for herself whether she is at increased risk. HRT patches are preferred if there is any increased risk of thrombosis, as they reduce the risk of developing a clot while on HRT.

Endometrial Cancer

This is a cancer which can develop in the lining of the womb or endometrium. It is a reasonably uncommon cancer, but it is seen in women who take oestrogen-only HRT when they still have an intact womb. This is because the oestrogen over-stimulates the womb. HRT preparations specifically for women with a womb are balanced with progestogen, so this risk is completely eliminated.

Premature Menopause

This is when your periods stop at 40 years of age or less. This happens to approximately 1 per cent of women under the age of 40 – more common than you might think. It is also known as premature ovarian insufficiency (POI), which is more accurate, as women in this age group can sometimes experience a temporary 'awakening' of the ovaries from time to time.

Causes of Premature Menopause

It is not very well understood why premature menopause happens to some women but there are a few theories, which are outlined below.

Autoimmune Diseases

Some women with autoimmune diseases which cause them to produce antibodies to an organ within their bodies, such as diabetes and hypothyroidism, are more at risk of producing antibodies to their ovaries, causing a premature menopause.

Genetic Factors

Some families have a history of premature menopause.

Chemotherapy/Radiotherapy/Surgical Removal of Ovaries

For some women undergoing treatments for cancer, the ovaries may be permanently damaged by the treatment, leading to early failure of the ovaries. Obviously if the ovaries are removed through surgery, menopause follows immediately.

This is often a devastating diagnosis for a younger woman, especially if they have not yet had any children. Your doctor may want to do an FSH test or an AMH test to confirm the diagnosis. FSH is produced by the brain and starts to rise when the ovaries are failing. AMH is produced by the ovaries and directly reflects the healthiness of your ovaries. If you are going through a premature menopause, your AMH level will be very low.

Treatment of Premature Menopause

The most important message for women who are going through this often traumatic time is that it is essential to replace the hormones that are deficient until the age of 50. This is to protect them from an early onset of bone density loss and heart disease. Using HRT in this group of women does not increase the risk of breast cancer – that is agreed by all experts worldwide. Often, higher doses are required to control a younger woman's symptoms, and vaginal oestrogen is often needed to allow the woman to continue a healthy sex life.

If fertility is an issue and pregnancy is desired, there are some options available to a woman who has experienced a premature menopause, and who still has an intact womb. Because the reserve of eggs in the ovaries has gone, eggs will need to be obtained from a donor, which can be used with sperm taken from the woman's partner or a sperm donor in an IVF procedure. The woman herself can safely carry the pregnancy, using some extra hormones in the initial stages. Adoption and surrogacy are two other options.

It is important to have regular checks with your doctor if you have been diagnosed with premature menopause. Your ongoing care should include:

- Twice-yearly check-ups for breast examination, blood pressure check and repeat HRT prescriptions
- Annual fasting bloods to check cholesterol and glucose levels
- DEXA bone scans every three to five years if they are normal

Conclusion

So there you have it. The menopause comes in all shapes and sizes, and every woman is different. There are lots of things you can do yourself to help get through it as easily as possible. You should talk to your doctor about your symptoms and your health in general. Look on the menopause as the beginning of a new phase in your life which is different, but not necessarily any less fulfilling, than your younger years. It certainly marks the beginning of a new stage in your general health, and you need to spend a little more time monitoring it. There are very successful, safe treatments available for you if you are finding that the menopause is affecting you to a significant degree. HRT is a safe and efficient option for relief of your menopausal symptoms, but not every woman will need it.

Checklist for Menopausal Women

- Mammograms from the age of 50 onwards (BreastCheck is a breast-screening programme available to women aged 50 to 64 which provides a free mammogram every two years)
- Cervical smears every five years (CervicalCheck, the National Cervical Screening Programme, provides free smear tests to women aged 25 to 60)
- Annual blood tests – fasting cholesterol and glucose, thyroid testing
- DEXA scan for osteoporosis at the onset of menopause, then every five years if the results are normal
- Weight management
- Regular exercise

Key Points

- The average age at which your periods stop is 50.
- The perimenopause starts much earlier, when your menstrual cycle starts to change.
- Symptoms of the menopause can be physical, psychological and emotional.
- Treatment options include diet and exercise, alternative therapies and HRT.
- Premature menopause occurs when your periods stop at the age of 40 or less.
- Long-term problems associated with the menopause include vaginal dryness and osteoporosis.
- HRT can be safely used in the 45 to 55-year-old age group for less than five years to relieve symptoms of the menopause.

14

Adolescent Gynaecology

The adolescent years can be difficult enough for everyone, both for a young girl and for her parents. When you add in sexual development, including the arrival of periods and the potential problems that can arise from them, it can be an even trickier time. The family GP who has looked after you since you were a baby may not be the person you want to talk to about a possibly embarrassing topic. Finding a doctor you can really talk to is half the battle, and keep reminding yourself – this is not embarrassing for your doctor!

This chapter will cover some of the more common problems that can arise in this age group, including:

- A delay in puberty
- Precocious puberty
- Period problems – heavy or irregular
- Acne

Delayed Puberty

Puberty is the word used to describe the time during which sexual maturation or development is achieved. In girls this is usually between 10 and 14 years of age. It is slightly later in boys – 12 to 16 years of age. The average age of puberty has reduced over the last one hundred years. This is thought to be at least partly due to the increased body weight of our children. A certain amount of body fat is required to trigger puberty, and that crucial amount seems to be reached earlier in more recent times.

Signs of Puberty and Delayed Puberty

The first sign of female puberty is usually breast development, followed by pubic hair development. In a small minority of girls, pubic hair will develop before breasts. Around this time, a girl's body shape will start to change, with fat being deposited on the upper and lower parts of the body, leading to a curvier appearance. Periods normally arrive two-and-a-half years after the onset of these changes. In girls whose periods start younger than 13 years of age, regular periods are usually established quite quickly. In those girls who do not start having periods until age 13 or later, they are much more likely to have irregular periods for up to four years after their first period. The 'growth spurt' happens usually six months before the first period. This period of intense growth can last for up to two years.

Delayed puberty is when:

- No breast development has occurred by the age of 13.
- No pubic hair growth has appeared by the age of 14.
- Periods have not started by the age of 15.

Causes of Delayed Puberty

The most common reason for a delay in puberty is known as a constitutional delay. This is when the rate of growth is slower in a child, slowing down from as early as 6 months of age. There is no reason for this, and it is a normal variation. The child will continue to grow at a slower rate than other children their age. Puberty is also delayed. These children always 'catch up' and will grow to a normal height. Constitutional delay accounts for about 25 per cent of all cases of delayed puberty, but other causes should be looked for.

Other causes of delayed puberty include:

- Familial – parents and other siblings who have also had delayed puberty
- Malnutrition – perhaps due to anorexia nervosa, coeliac disease or cystic fibrosis
- Chronic illnesses, such as Crohn's disease, kidney disease, diabetes and underactive or overactive thyroid disease
- Genetic disorders, such as Turner syndrome, where one X chromosome is missing and the ovaries never develop properly

Diagnosis of Delayed Puberty

Your doctor should take a history regarding the pattern of growth, any chronic illnesses, any family history of delayed puberty, and so on. Examination should include measured height and weight, taking note of any features of puberty; the height of the parents should also be documented.

Investigations can include x-rays of the fingers, hand and wrist, which assess the bone age of the child. The bone age of the child can predict the eventual height of the child as an adult, and diagnose constitutional delay as the cause of delayed puberty.

Other investigations can include blood tests to look for any illnesses such as kidney disease and coeliac disease, hormone levels to check for thyroid and ovary function, and chemicals produced in the brain – FSH and LH – which control the ovaries in later life. Analysis of chromosomes may be needed.

Treatment of Delayed Puberty

Most cases of delayed puberty require no treatment, and reassurance and monitoring is sufficient. Other causes of delayed puberty need to be treated according to their needs.

Precocious Puberty

This is the term given to the appearance of signs of puberty before the age of 8. Precocious puberty is much more common in girls than in boys. In many cases of precocious puberty in girls there is no underlying cause. Childhood obesity is thought to be the cause of some cases. However, a thyroid or ovarian hormone problem, a genetic cause, head injury or brain tumour can also be responsible for these symptoms.

In the case of an underlying condition, treatment of this will resolve the precocious puberty symptoms. In other cases where no underlying cause is found, medication called GnRH agonists can be given, which blocks any further sex hormone production until a more appropriate age.

Period Problems

What Is Normal and What Is Not Normal?

In adolescent girls, normal variation on the length of a menstrual cycle is 21 to 45 days. The period should last for no longer than seven days. It is difficult to know whether your periods are heavier than everyone else's. A general rule of thumb is that changing pads or tampons every hour (because they are soaked, not for comfort reasons) for the first few days of your period probably indicates that your periods are heavier than most. Another sign of heavy flow is soaking through during the night and staining the bed linen. Passing large blood clots is also a sign of heavy menstrual flow. In

terms of period pain, your period should not stop you from participating in sports, social activities and so on. Often, doctors use the
presence of missed days from school as a good way of determining
how severe period pain is.

Period problems can be quite common in this age group. Periods
can be irregular, painful or heavy, or all of the above! As mentioned
earlier, periods can be irregular for the first few years after the onset
of periods, especially if the girl is a little older when her periods
start. This irregularity is usually due to what is known as anovulatory cycles. These are cycles that last longer than 45 days (i.e. the
number of days from day 1 of a period to day 1 of the next period)
and usually mean that no egg is released from the ovaries during the
menstrual cycle. This leads to longer cycles, with a thicker lining of
the womb developing. This eventually leads to a heavier and painful
period.

In some girls the cycle becomes regular quickly, but they become
progressively more painful. This is known as primary dysmenorrhoea (see Chapter 9).

In some girls the periods are consistently very heavy from the
onset of menstruation. Because this is not a topic that daughters
particularly want to discuss in great detail with their parents or
friends, they assume that this is normal and occasionally it is only
when the girl develops anaemia that the true heaviness of the
periods comes to light. In these cases a blood test to check that
there is no clotting problem may be appropriate.

An inherited condition called von Willebrand disease can present
as heavy periods in adolescent girls, where the girl's blood does
not clot efficiently, leading to extremely heavy periods. However,
it should be noted that in 95 per cent of cases of young girls with
very heavy periods, the reason is simply anovulatory cycles.

Your doctor should be able to ask the appropriate questions to
establish what the best treatment should be. No examination should
be necessary in most cases.

Treatments for Period Problems

- NSAIDs – this is a group of medications, the most well-known being mefanamic acid or Ponstan. This is excellent at controlling pain associated with periods, and also makes periods lighter. However, it has no effect on the regularity of periods. It should be taken prior to the onset of bleeding and three times daily on the most painful days of the period. Regular use greatly improves its effectiveness, rather than just using it when the pain is at its maximum.

- Oral contraceptive pill – this is commonly used in this age group for periods which are proving disruptive to a girl's life, such as interfering with school attendance, sports, and so on. This form of treatment establishes a regular, light period within a very short time. Usually, period pain is also sufficiently controlled but, if not, NSAIDs can be used with it.

- In some cases where the oral contraceptive pill is not wanted by the patient or her parents, progestogens (a non-contraceptive hormone tablet) can be given for ten to fourteen days every month. This brings about a regular, lighter, less painful period.

Acne

Acne affects up to 20 per cent of all adolescent girls. This can range from a mild form right through to devastatingly severe acne. Contrary to popular belief, acne has little if anything to do with diet. Increased hormone production and the resultant effect on the production of sebum (an oily substance produced within the pores in the skin), as well as bacterial infection, are much more important considerations. In adolescence the increased production of androgens (male hormones), albeit in small amounts in girls, can be enough to spark off acne. If there are other signs of too much androgen production (such as facial hair growth and irregular or absent periods), your doctor should consider the diagnosis of poly-cystic ovarian syndrome (see Chapter 9).

Treatments for Acne

Various treatments can be tried depending on the severity of the acne. The main thing to remember is that no young girl should have to live with bad acne in this day and age. There are lots of different options to treat it, and if one doesn't work, try another.

Topical Treatments

These are treatments that are applied directly to the skin. One of the best is benzoyl peroxide, particularly when combined with an antibiotic such as clindamycin within the topical treatment. Benzoyl peroxide acts as an antiseptic, but it also helps to clear the blocked pore and reduce redness from inflammation. This is best used in mild cases of acne, or in the long term for maintaining good skin after stopping another treatment which has been used in the short term. Side effects include mild redness for a while after application, so it is recommended that you apply it at night.

Oral Antibiotics

These are useful for treating acne which is a little more advanced. They work by killing off any bacteria causing the acne. Common antibiotics used include tetracycline, minocycline and doxycycline. The length of treatment varies according to your response. Usually an improvement is seen within four weeks, but it is generally recommended to continue taking the antibiotics for up to four months or until the skin is perfect. Side effects can include indigestion and skin pigmentation.

Oral Contraceptive Pill

This is very useful in controlling acne in adolescent girls. It reduces male hormone or androgen production, and this directly reduces the oiliness of the skin.

Isotretinoin (Roaccutane)

This drug is part of a family of drugs, derived from vitamin A. It works by dramatically reducing the production of sebum in the skin. This is used in more severe cases of acne, which have not responded to any of the above treatments, or when scarring is a risk. It is prescribed under the supervision of a dermatologist (skin specialist). This is because it is a very strong medication, and the patient needs to be carefully monitored while taking it. Blood tests to check your liver need to be done at intervals while taking Roaccutane. The average length of treatment is approximately 16 to 24 weeks, and repeat treatments are rarely needed. Side effects include dry lips and eyes, and hypersensitivity to sunlight, requiring SPF 15 at all times. It is also very harmful to unborn foetuses, and contraception is essential in sexually active adolescents while using Roaccutane.

Key Points

- The average age of puberty in girls is 10 to 14 years.
- A growth spurt usually happens six months before the first period.
- In most cases of delayed puberty no cause is found.
- The most common cause of heavy periods in adolescent girls is anovulatory cycles.
- Creams, oral antibiotics and the oral contraceptive pill can be used to effectively treat acne.

15

Mental Health Problems

Anxiety

Anxiety is one of those conditions which sneak up on women without them realising it. Everyone feels anxious at times, and this is a totally normal feeling to experience. However, when you are feeling anxious more days than not, or experiencing physical symptoms caused directly by anxiety, then you may be developing generalised anxiety disorder (GAD).

GAD is thought to affect about 5 per cent of women, and is twice as common in women than in men. GAD is a group of conditions, which include phobias, social anxiety and obsessive compulsive disorder, as well as a generalised, non-specific anxiety. Anxiety can be defined as a mood disorder that typically involves multiple and/ or non-specific worries that interfere with the person's life in some way. Usually, if you experiencing anxiety symptoms most days over a six-month period, with at least three of the physical symptoms being experienced on a regular basis, a diagnosis of anxiety can be made. Most women with anxiety will report that their anxiety is having a negative impact on their ability to function at work, college and in relationships. They will also report that despite their best efforts, they cannot control their worrying.

Risk Factors for Developing Anxiety

There are certain factors which increase your risk of developing anxiety. These include:

- Being female
- Age – being a young adult rather than an older adult
- Family history of depression or anxiety
- Health problems
- Family disagreements

Signs and Symptoms of Anxiety

Signs and symptoms to watch out for include:

- Feeling 'on edge'
- Tiredness
- Difficulty sleeping
- Trouble with concentrating
- Irritability
- Muscle tension

In the case of specific phobias, you may find that you are avoiding certain situations to avoid causing a heightening of your anxiety levels. When anxiety levels escalate, panic attacks may occur, which are both frightening and debilitating. Signs and symptoms of these include:

- Sweating
- Nausea
- Palpitations (sensation of your heart beating very fast)
- Chest tightness
- Shortness of breath

- Shaking or trembling
- Difficulty breathing
- A sense that something terrible is going to happen to you
- Numbness or tingling

It is important to exclude any other cause for the anxiety, including it being part of another psychiatric illness, such as schizophrenia, or due to illegal drug use. An overactive thyroid gland can also mimic the symptoms of anxiety, and your doctor may do a simple blood test to check for this.

How to Treat Anxiety

There are two main ways to treat anxiety – medication and psycho-therapy – and in a lot of cases the two types of treatment are combined.

Medication

A group of drugs called selective serotonin re-uptake inhibitors (SSRIs) and serotonin-noradrenaline re-uptake inhibitor (SNRIs) are commonly used to treat anxiety. They work by increasing the levels of serotonin and noradrenaline in the brain. These medica-tions take up to four weeks to take effect.

Benzodiazepines can be used for short-term relief of anxiety and can be very useful. In particular, alprazolam (Xanax) is used for the control of panic attacks, as it acts quickly. However, this group of drugs is highly addictive and must be used with caution. Your doctor will explain to you that these can only be prescribed in small amounts, and used only if necessary. In fact it is often the case that knowing you have a fast-acting medication to hand that you could use if needed provides enough reassurance to reduce your anxiety levels without actually having to take the drug.

Beta blockers are a group of drugs used primarily in treating high blood pressure. Propranolol (Inderal) can be used to successfully treat the physical symptoms associated with panic attacks.

Psychotherapy

Psychotherapy has been shown to be as effective, if not more so, than medication. The most common type used in the treatment of anxiety is cognitive behavioural therapy (CBT). This type of therapy is designed to help the patient identify and decrease the irrational thoughts and behaviours that worsen their anxiety. The basis of CBT is that your own thoughts – not other people or situations – determine how you feel or behave. Therefore, by changing your thinking to a more positive outlook you can improve your situation, even if the situation itself is unchanged. Other changes to behaviour which can be helpful are relaxation techniques and gradual exposure to situations which would have previously provoked a lot of anxiety. Another useful tool is to help the patient understand where the physical symptoms of anxiety arise from, which can help them control them.

Self-help

Avoidance of alcohol, caffeine and illegal drugs are all important to help you recover from an anxiety disorder. Other relaxation techniques, such as aerobic exercise, yoga and meditation have all been shown to help.

Improvement in anxiety levels is usually seen over a period of six to eight weeks after treatment is started. Usually your doctor will suggest staying on medication for about six months, with CBT sessions becoming less frequent until they are no longer required. Anxiety medication needs to be stopped slowly, under your doctor's guidance, to avoid unwanted side effects.

Depression

Depression is an illness which causes enormous disruption to people's lives: both their own and their loved ones'. Because of the stigma of mental illness in Ireland it continues to be under-reported and under-diagnosed. The truth is, it is not a weakness or something you can 'snap out of'; it is an illness that needs to be treated.

It is usually defined as a persistent feeling of sadness and loss of interest. It can also cause physical symptoms. There are lots of different types of depression, including postnatal depression; depression associated with episodes of mania, called bipolar disorder; and reactive depression, which is the natural reaction to a sudden loss, often of a loved one. However, the most common form of depression is called endogenous depression, clinical depression or major depression, and this is what is being described below.

Symptoms of Depression

Common symptoms of depression include:

- Feelings of sadness
- Loss of interest in usual activities
- Irritability
- Reduced sex drive
- Inability to sleep, waking early or excessive sleeping
- Changes in appetite – resulting in weight loss or weight gain
- Tiredness
- Poor concentration
- Feelings of worthlessness or guilt
- Unexplained physical symptoms such as backache or headache

Why Does Depression Occur?

The following are some of the many reasons why depression can occur:

- Depression runs in families; a genetic link is still being investigated.
- Neurotransmitters – these brain chemicals are related to our mood and changes in their levels can cause depression.
- Hormones – a hormonal imbalance with female hormones, thyroid hormone and others can cause or trigger depression.
- Early childhood trauma – adults who have experienced early childhood trauma are more likely to develop depression.
- Life events – loss or death of a loved one or financial difficulties can trigger depression.

What Are the Risk Factors for Developing Depression?

Certain factors increase your risk of developing depression. These include:

- Being female
- Being a young adult
- History of a traumatic childhood
- History of previous depression
- Family history of depression
- Being socially isolated, with few friends or family
- Having a serious illness
- Using alcohol or illegal drugs
- Having certain personality traits, such as low self-esteem

Diagnosis of Depression

Apart from suffering from depression itself, depression can be associated with other complications, such as alcohol and drug abuse, social isolation, financial difficulties, conflict within the family, relationship breakdown, anxiety and suicide. In order for your doctor to diagnose depression, they need to ask you in detail about your mood and emotions, your thoughts and behaviour patterns. You will be asked about any thoughts of suicide or self-harm you may have had. Your doctor may even ask you to complete a questionnaire to see if your symptoms are severe enough to be considered as depression.

Treatment of Depression

Like anxiety, the mainstay of treatment for depression is medication and cognitive behavioural therapy (CBT). Some doctors believe psychotherapy alone is sufficient; others believe that in order to bring someone with depression to a point where they can benefit from psychotherapy, medication is required. It is also thought that medication works more quickly, thereby preventing any further worsening of mood. It is known that the worse the depression episode, the more difficult and longer it is to treat.

Medication

SSRIs are the most commonly used medications to treat depression. This is mostly because of their effectiveness in treating depression, but also because of the few side effects for patients while taking them. SSRIs include venlafaxine (Effexor), escitalopram (Lexapro), sertraline (Lustral), duloxetine (Cymbalta), citalopram (Cipramil), and paroxetine (Seroxat). They work by increasing serotonin levels in the brain, which positively affects mood. They take several weeks to take full effect, and have some side effects, such as insomnia, dry mouth, restlessness, loss of libido, nausea and diarrhoea. However, most of these side effects are only present initially. It is recommended that they be taken for a minimum of nine to twelve months to get the full benefit from the medication, and to minimise the risk of the depression recurring. SSRIs, like other medications, should not be stopped suddenly without consultation with your doctor. Marked side effects can occur, such as agitation and flu-like symptoms.

Psychotherapy

CBT is the most useful form of psychotherapy for treating depression. Indeed, in cases of mild depression it may be sufficient without medication. In cases of severe depression CBT should be part of the treatment, in conjunction with medication. The therapist helps the patient identify negative thoughts and behaviours, and change them to a healthier pattern. This is based on the concept that consistently negative thought patterns affect mood and behaviour. The process of CBT is a learning process for the patient, and involves active participation by the patient, who is often given tasks to complete between sessions. Coping skills are also taught, to help the patient resolve problems which would have previously proved difficult as a result of depression. CBT usually lasts for twelve to sixteen sessions, depending on the patient's progress.

Self-help Measures

Depression is a serious illness, and you should always talk to your doctor if you are worried that you may be suffering from it, rather than trying to cope with it on your own. Remember, true clinical depression tends to get worse rather than better, and the worse it gets, the longer it can take to get better, so early treatment is very important. Natural remedies such as St John's Wort are used widely by patients who are treating themselves for depression. It is important to remember that although it is a naturally-occurring substance, it is still a powerful medication and you should always consult your doctor before using it.

Below are a few recommendations about how to help yourself while your doctor is treating you for depression.

Learn About Depression

It is really important to know all about your illness. This will allow you to understand your symptoms and help you explain what you are going through to your friends and family.

Pay Attention to Warning Signs

If you feel that your symptoms are returning or worsening on treatment, tell your doctor straight away.

Stick to Your Treatment Plan

Don't be tempted to stop your treatment early because you are feeling well again. Trust your doctor that they are doing the right thing for you, and if you do want to try something different talk to them first.

Get Exercise

Exercise is well recognised as a way of improving mood.

Avoid Alcohol and Illegal Drugs

Alcohol and drugs worsen depression and should be avoided when being treated. People with depression often use alcohol and drugs to escape from their emotions, or to help with their insomnia. However, both are natural depressants and will worsen the situation.

Get Plenty of Sleep

Tiredness will worsen depression, so getting as much sleep as possible is important.

Alcohol Abuse and Alcoholism

Alcohol abuse and alcoholism in women is probably underestimated in Ireland, and it is a growing problem. Four out of every ten women are drinking alcohol at a level which is thought to have a negative effect on their wellbeing. Irish female teenagers are now drinking the same amounts as their male counterparts. From the female perspective, it is much easier for a woman to develop alcohol-related health problems, such as liver damage.

What Is the Difference Between Alcohol Abuse and Alcoholism?

With alcohol abuse, you may not be dependent on alcohol but you are drinking excessive amounts, and it is having a negative effect on your life in general. Alcoholism is a chronic disease where your body is dependent on alcohol. With both alcoholism and alcohol abuse you may not be able to stop without help.

What Are the Symptoms of Alcohol Abuse and Alcoholism?

- A strong need to drink alcohol
- Increasing tolerance to alcohol; in other words, increasing amounts of alcohol are required to feels its effects
- An inability to limit the amount of alcohol consumed
- Financial, legal or relationship problems as a result of alcohol
- Drinking alone or in secret
- Symptoms of withdrawal from alcohol – sweating, nausea and shaking – when you don't drink
- Losing interest in activities that you previously enjoyed
- Blackouts – unable to remember conversations, etc. due to alcohol
- Gulping drinks or ordering doubles

With alcohol abuse many of these symptoms will be present, but the craving for alcohol or withdrawal symptoms may not be.

Drinking Responsibly

The quantity of alcohol which a woman should not exceed is 14 units per week, but the units should be spread out over the week, rather than a large number of units being consumed at one sitting. Typical measures of alcohol can be broken down into units as follows:

- One medium glass of wine (175 ml) = 2 units of alcohol
- One glass of beer = 1 unit of alcohol
- One pint of beer = 2 units of alcohol
- One single measure of spirits = 1 unit of alcohol

Therefore, the practical recommendation for women is to drink no more than 2 to 3 units of alcohol per day, with several alcohol-free days during the week.

Alcohol dependence happens over time. Chemicals within alcohol affect the balance of other chemicals within the brain which control the pleasurable effects of alcohol. Over time, increasing amounts of alcohol are required to achieve a similar effect. Although alcohol can be enjoyed in moderation and as part of a healthy lifestyle, it is important to monitor your drinking and to ensure that you do not regularly drink to excess.

What Are the Risk Factors for Developing Alcoholism?

- Gender – men are more likely to become dependent on alcohol, but women are more likely to develop alcohol-related health problems.
- Prolonged high alcohol intake over time

- Family history of alcohol abuse
- Personal history of abuse as a child
- Mental illness
- Starting to drink alcohol at a young age greatly increases your risk of becoming dependent on alcohol.

Complications of Alcoholism

- Increased risk of accidents or suicide
- Liver disease
- Heart disease
- Pancreas and stomach problems
- Eye complications, including weakness of the eye muscles
- Neurological problems
- Increased risk of cancer
- Diabetes
- Osteoporosis
- Birth defects

How to Diagnose Alcohol Abuse and Alcoholism

Your doctor will be able to judge from talking to you whether you are abusing alcohol or, indeed, whether you are an alcoholic. Denial is a large part of this illness, however, and it is common for friends and family to bring your unhealthy drinking habits to your attention, rather than for you to independently seek out help from your doctor. If you think you are abusing alcohol but are not physically addicted yet, you should still see your doctor. They can help you seek out help, in the form of a support group like Alcoholics Anonymous or a counsellor.

There are criteria for diagnosing alcoholism, of which you should have been experiencing at least three over the previous twelve months. These include:

- Tolerance – needing more and more drinks to achieve the same effect
- Drinking more than you intended
- Withdrawal symptoms when you don't drink, such as shaking, sweating, feeling sick, etc.
- Wanting to control your drinking habits but not being able to
- Spending large amounts of time drinking and recovering from alcohol
- No longer participating in activities that you previously would have enjoyed

There are no physical tests that will help your doctor diagnose an alcohol problem, but they may want to do some tests to check for any damage caused by excessive drinking.

Treatment of Alcohol Abuse and Alcoholism

If you are not dependent on alcohol, simply cutting down on your alcohol intake will be sufficient. However, if you are addicted to alcohol, then this will not work – alcohol must be removed forever from your life. This can be done through various means:

- Detoxification and withdrawal. This is usually done when you are an in-patient in an alcohol treatment centre. Withdrawal itself lasts for four to seven days, and medication is given to help with the symptoms of withdrawal.
- Learning new behaviours and using them in a new long-term plan which includes avoiding alcohol permanently
- Counselling to help discover why you were so dependent on a drug like alcohol, and to provide ongoing support
- Taking medication such as disulfiram (Antabus) – a tablet that can be used by recovering alcoholics to help their willpower in avoiding alcohol. If alcohol is taken with Antabus, severe

symptoms, such as flushing, vomiting and sweats, will follow. This has no effect on the craving associated with recovering from alcoholism.

- Long-term support – after discharge from a stay at a treatment centre, aftercare is part of the ongoing support system for the patient. This includes group or individual counselling, and Alcoholics Anonymous, where recovering alcoholics meet regularly to support each other.
- Professional psychological/psychiatric care if the alcoholism is associated with any ongoing mental health issues, such as depression. Medication and ongoing psychological assessment may be needed.

Anorexia

Anorexia is a mental illness which is potentially life threatening. It most commonly starts in adolescence when girls between the ages of 14 and 18 attempt to control their weight and restrict what they eat in an attempt to lose weight. Sufferers of anorexia usually have a distorted view of their body shape. They often exercise excessively, and go to great lengths to hide their weight loss from their family and friends. Binge eating is a feature for some girls, where they eat a large amount of food at one time, followed by a period of abstinence from food. Purging (causing themselves to vomit and using laxatives) can also be a problem.

Signs and Symptoms of Anorexia

Some of the typical behaviour of an anorexic girl or woman can include:

- Missing meals
- Only eating certain low-calorie foods in your presence, such as lettuce or celery

222

- Making repeated claims that they have already eaten
- Complaining of being fat, even though they have a normal weight or are underweight
- Repeatedly weighing themselves and looking at themselves in the mirror
- Excessive exercising
- Avoiding situations where they may be expected to eat
- Wearing baggy, loose clothes to hide their body shape

Physical signs of anorexia can include:

- Extreme weight loss
- An increase of fine body hair and facial hair
- Poor condition of teeth and bad breath (from vomiting)
- Periods stopping completely
- Excessive tiredness

What Causes Anorexia?

There are many theories as to why some women and girls develop anorexia; some of these include:

- Psychological/basic personality traits – a basic tendency towards anxiety and depression, poor coping skills to deal with stress, and a need for perfectionism
- External factors – a perceived need to be thin reinforced by media, bereavement, bullying, sexual or physical abuse

Diagnosing Anorexia

One of the biggest challenges facing anorexia sufferers and their families is getting help. Often if you are anorexic you are resistant to help, and sometimes you do not even realise there is a problem. You deny there has been significant weight loss. Your doctor will ask a series of questions to establish whether you have a normal relationship with food, and your typical exercise routine. Usually girls with anorexia are 15 per cent below the average weight for their height, and their BMI is usually 17.5 or lower.

Treatment Options for Anorexia

Treatment usually involves a combination of talking therapy and dietary planning. The aim is to slowly put weight back on, normally at a rate of 1 lb per week. In most cases, this is achieved as an outpatient. Admission to hospital to treat anorexia is a last resort, when the patient's life is thought to be in danger.

On average, anorexia sufferers take up to five years to recover. It is a sad fact that the risk of relapsing is quite high with anorexia, and it is a leading cause of death from a mental health illness.

Bulimia

This is another form of eating disorder, where an abnormal relationship with food exists. Bulimia typically affects girls at an older age, usually in the late teens. Bulimic girls restrict their food intake dramatically, and then eat large amounts of high calorie food without control, followed by an episode of purging, either with forced vomiting or laxative use. Bingeing and purging are followed by feelings of guilt and low self-esteem, with the cycle of restricted food intake starting again as a form of self-punishment. The frequency of binges increases quite quickly. Often the binges are associated with times of emotional stress and anxiety.

Signs and Symptoms of Bulimia

Signs of bulimia (in yourself and others) include:

- An obsessive attitude towards food
- Being overcritical of one's weight

- Leaving the table shortly after eating (to vomit in secret), then appearing flushed with scarred knuckles (from induced vomiting)
- Regular changes in weight
- Depression and anxiety
- Scarred knuckles
- Poor condition of teeth

Diagnosis and Treatment of Bulimia

Treatment of bulimia first involves talking to your doctor, and acknowledging that you need help. Treatment usually includes talking therapy, in particular CBT to help you to think more positively about yourself and life in general. Antidepressants and anti-anxiety medication, such as SSRIs, may be very helpful in your recovery process. This is not a quick recovery process – bulimia can take years to be successfully treated, as so much of the treatment involves changing your behaviour and your thinking towards food and yourself as a person.

Key Points

- Anxiety and depression are common conditions in women; both can be treated with medication, psychotherapy or a combination of both.
- Alcoholism has devastating physical and psychological effects, especially in women.
- Treatment options include detoxification, counselling, alcohol avoidance medication and ongoing support from family, friends and professionals.
- Anorexia and bulimia are seen increasingly in adolescent girls and young women, and require a lot of treatment and support in order to recover.

16

Sexual Problems

Sexual problems are most certainly underestimated in women. In some surveys it is estimated that 40 per cent of women experience sexual difficulty at some stage in their lives, the most common reasons being lack of sex drive and pain with sex. Painful sex is known as dyspareunia. There are times in a woman's life when these changes can be expected and are normal, but prolonged sexual problems should be addressed. The reality is that a lot of women suffer in silence, due to embarrassment. This should never be the case – all women are entitled to a satisfying and enjoyable sex life, and any problems preventing this should be dealt with in a sensitive way.

Pain with Sex

Pain with sex can be divided into two types:

- Pain on entry – this is known as superficial dyspareunia.
- Pain on deep penetration – this is known as deep dyspareunia.

Superficial Dyspareunia

This can happen for several reasons, which have been dealt with in other chapters, including the following:

- Vaginal dryness due to low oestrogen levels (see Chapter 13)
- Vaginal or vulval infections (see Chapter 17)
- Skin conditions, such as eczema or thrush
- Surgery to the vagina, such as an episiotomy during childbirth
- Vaginismus
- Vaginal dryness due to low libido

Vaginismus

Vaginismus can be described as either a complete inability to have vaginal penetration, or pain, burning or stinging in association with penetration. This is brought about by a complex process which involves both the vaginal muscles at the opening to the vagina, and the brain. It can be primary or secondary. Most vaginismus is primary, i.e. it has always been present since first sexual activity was attempted. Secondary vaginismus is less common, where a perfectly normal, satisfactory sex life was present before becoming painful and difficult. This is seen with the onset of the menopause, infections such as chronic thrush, and traumatic childbirth.

How Common is Vaginismus?

Vaginismus is a common vaginal condition which affects large numbers of women. It is estimated that 2 per cent of all women will have some degree of vaginismus during their lifetime, although this figure could be even higher, as sexual problems are generally under-reported to doctors due to embarrassment on the part of the patient. Vaginismus causes extreme distress to women for obvious reasons, and can have far-reaching consequences for relationships if it is not addressed.

What Causes Vaginismus?

Causes of primary vaginismus are varied, and often the woman herself cannot identify a cause. Frequently, it is as simple as a woman's first sexual encounter being less than ideal: possibly without sufficient lubrication, or having been coerced into having sex for the first time without being really willing; or due to inadequate contraception and a fear of subsequent pregnancy. Other causes which have been suggested include childhood sexual abuse and a negative attitude towards sex instilled from childhood.

Vaginismus does not automatically mean an inability to become sexually aroused. Many women can have orgasms from clitoral stimulation but cannot progress to vaginal penetration. A lot of women with mild vaginismus can have cervical smears and can use tampons. However, with a lot of younger women for whom vaginal penetration is impossible, any genital contact is difficult and tampon use and cervical smears are impossible.

A cycle of events occurs with vaginismus which brings about the typical pattern of behaviour. Firstly, the woman starts to develop a conscious fear and anxiety as penetration seems imminent; the body then becomes tense and automatically tightens the vaginal muscles; the tightness that follows makes penetration impossible or painful; further pain causes more intense muscle tightening; finally, the woman will try to avoid intimacy and libido may fall. Pain from attempted sex can last for several days, and tearing of the skin at the entrance to the vagina can occur. Natural lubrication can be greatly reduced if the woman is tense, leading to soreness and chaffing inside the vagina for several days afterwards.

What Can I Do if I Have Vaginismus?

The most important step to take if you think this might be something that affects you is to seek appropriate help. This is not a condition that all doctors are going to be able to help you with. A doctor with a specific interest in women's health is a good place to start. Your doctor should take a full history from you, and then perform a limited examination, depending on your own comfort.

Occasionally, women who have what sounds like vaginismus may have a small piece of skin at the opening to the vagina, which is a remnant of the hymen. The hymen is a piece of tissue within the vagina which you are born with, and is designed to break down easily with first intercourse. Often, this breaks down before that with physical activity in childhood. In some cases, the tissue is thick and does not break down completely, causing painful sex. This can be detected by simple examination of the vagina, and is treated with a simple surgical procedure. However, it is important to remember that this is unusual, and by far the most common reason for difficulty with penetration is vaginismus. Women often report feeling like 'there is a wall' at the vaginal entrance, but this is just intense muscle spasm.

Treatment of vaginismus is highly successful but does require some work, both from the woman herself and her partner if she is in a relationship. The best approach to vaginismus usually involves a combination of complete understanding of vaginismus itself, examination of some psychological issues which may be at play, pelvic floor relaxation techniques, vaginal dilator exercises, controlled sensual work as a couple and, finally, preparation for penetration. These steps need to be followed in a controlled, non-hurried fashion, so that there is no progression to the next step until you are completely happy that you are fully relaxed with what you are doing. Sometimes working with a psychosexual therapist also helps, particularly if there is difficulty with all aspects of sexuality, as a more psychological approach initially may be more beneficial.

Deep Dyspareunia

This is pain on deep penetration, and is often associated with a pelvic problem, unlike superficial dyspareunia. Deep dyspareunia is also more likely to be a new symptom for women who have had a pain-free sex life until recently.

Causes

Possible causes of deep dyspareunia include:

- Endometriosis
- Ovarian cyst
- Uterine fibroid
- Tilted uterus
- Pelvic inflammatory disease
- Scarring from previous surgery, such as a caesarean section

Diagnosis

Your doctor will need to ask you lots of difficult questions which you may find embarrassing, but they are very important to try and establish what the cause for your pain is. These include where your pain is and whether it is present with every sexual position and with all previous sexual partners; you will also be asked about previous pelvic surgery or pelvic infections.

An examination can be very helpful in trying to make a diagnosis, but if you find the examination painful or difficult in any way you should let your doctor know that you do not wish to continue. Examining the outside of the vagina, as well as a pelvic and speculum examination, should help your doctor decide how best to help you. A pelvic ultrasound may be needed to further investigate your deep pelvic pain.

Low Sex Drive (Libido)

Libido is the word given to a woman's sexual desire, or her sex drive. It is a subject which rarely comes up for discussion between a woman and her doctor. It is difficult to estimate how big a problem low libido actually is, but it may be that as many as 40 per cent of all women experience sexual difficulty at some stage in their lives, and a low sex drive is the most common of these difficulties.

A woman's libido varies at different times in her life, depending on her relationships, as well as life-changing events like illness, menopause and pregnancy. Some medications can also cause your sex drive to be low. If your libido is consistently low over a few months, then you should talk to your doctor.

However, it should be clear that a low libido is only a problem if it is unwanted. For some women, having a low sex drive is not a problem and they are quite happy.

There is no 'normal' level of libido for women – it varies naturally from woman to woman, and there is a natural decline with age. The thing to remember is – if your lack of desire is bothering you, then you should talk to a professional.

What Causes a Low Libido in Women?

The truth is, there are many factors involved, and it can be difficult to identify what is the main culprit. Sometimes it is as easy as changing your medication and the problem is solved. In other cases it may be several factors interacting together, such as a breastfeeding mother with vaginal dryness secondary to hormone changes and extreme exhaustion.

Physical Causes

- General illness, e.g. diabetes, arthritis, and so on, will affect your libido

- Sexual problems, e.g. pain during sex
- Alcohol and drugs
- Medications, e.g. combined oral contraceptive pills, antidepressants and anti-convulsants used in epilepsy
- Exhaustion, e.g. newly-delivered mothers
- Surgery to breasts or genital area

Hormonal Causes

- Menopause – at the time of the menopause, oestrogen and testosterone levels drop, both of which contribute to libido. In addition, the vaginal dryness caused by low oestrogen levels will cause pain during sex, leading to a reduced desire.
- Pregnancy and breastfeeding – hormone levels contribute to loss of libido, especially during breastfeeding when vaginal dryness can be an issue due to low oestrogen levels. However, body image issues and sheer exhaustion will all contribute towards a low libido at this time.

Psychological Causes

These are as significant as physical causes for women, and can include:

- Mental health problems, such as depression or anxiety
- History of physical or sexual abuse
- Low self-esteem
- Poor body image
- Stress – this could be financial or work-related
- Cultural issues – if you have been brought up in an environment where sex is not a normal and healthy part of a woman's life

Relationship Causes

Women need a healthy, sharing relationship in order to enjoy intimacy with their partner, and the following relationship problems may contribute to a low libido:

- Unfaithfulness
- Poor communication
- Unresolved conflicts

How to Treat a Low Libido

The best approach to treating a low libido in women is to try to ascertain the cause or causes of their problem, and address these. This could include referral for specialist sexual therapy, relationship counselling, hormone therapy or changing medication.

Altering of Medication

Discussion with your doctor may lead them to change your medication to a different type. This is particularly true for antidepressants. A change in your method of contraception may also be worth considering. It is very important never to suddenly stop taking your medication – always consult your doctor first.

Hormone Therapy

Oestrogen therapy in the form of a tablet or patch may help with a low libido, by improving mood and energy levels as well as improving the condition of the vagina. Vaginal oestrogen which is delivered directly into the vagina using a cream or tablet works well at reversing the dryness associated with the menopause. Women produce small amounts of testosterone in the ovaries before the menopause; testosterone patches or gels can be used and can work well to restore a woman's libido, particularly after the menopause.

Counselling

This can be very helpful for psychological causes of low libido. Counselling can be done with your partner, or as an individual, and can help you figure out what psychological issues are preventing you from enjoying a healthy sex life. For couples, sexual therapy may also help to improve desire by enhancing your experiences through better techniques.

What Can I Do to Help My Libido?

Things you can do to help improve your low libido include the following:
- Exercise, which boosts your mood and improves body image, can improve your libido.
- Stress management – find techniques to reduce your stress, such as meditation or yoga.
- Communicate better with your partner – set aside time to talk to each other in a meaningful way, away from the stresses of everyday life.
- Book time together for intimacy – set aside time when you can completely relax with each other and be intimate; show your partner that sex is important to you by putting aside some quality time.

Key Points

- Painful sex can be classified as superficial or deep.
- Common causes of superficial painful sex include dryness and vaginismus.
- Treatment of vaginismus involves both physical and psychological aspects.

- Deep painful sex is more likely to be associated with a pelvic problem, such as endometriosis.
- Libido in women is affected by physical, psychological and emotional factors.

17

Vaginal and Vulval Problems

Ask any woman if she has ever had a 'problem' in the vaginal area at some stage in her life and the answer will invariably be yes. Most vaginal complaints are simple, common and easy to treat. However, due to the intimate and personal nature of this area of our bodies, it can be difficult to discuss this with your doctor. If you then add in the extra factor of sexual difficulty and pain associated with sex, it becomes a very awkward visit to the doctor indeed. Please remember that your doctor is familiar with most sexual problems, and is never embarrassed by anything a patient may tell them. All they want to do is help, so don't be afraid to ask for help. I have covered the most common complaints involving the vagina and vulva below.

Thrush

This common infection is caused by a fungus – *Candida albicans*. This condition is also known as vulvovaginal candidiasis, as it usually causes vaginal and vulval symptoms. About 20 per cent of all women have *Candida albicans* in their vagina, which is perfectly normal and will not cause them any problems. *Candida* thrives in an environment which is rich in oestrogen, so the infection is most commonly seen in women aged 15 to 55. An overgrowth of *Candida* will lead to symptoms of thick white discharge, soreness or burning within the vagina, especially aggravated by sex, and a rash and itch on the vulval area, which can extend to around the anal area.

Female Genital Area

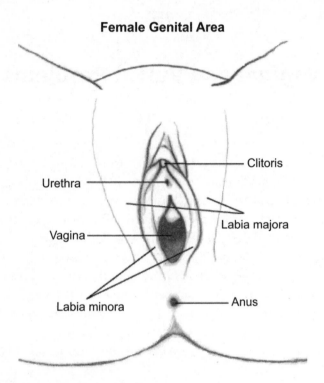

Risk Factors for Developing Thrush

Some predisposing factors to vulvovaginal candidiasis include:

- Pregnancy
- Diabetes
- Antibiotic usage
- Iron deficiency anaemia

Diagnosis of Thrush

Diagnosis of vulvovaginal candidiasis is based on examination of the patient, although in some cases a swab taken from the top of the vagina using a speculum is helpful to differentiate it from other vaginal infections. The appearance of thrush is that of a red rash which can affect either part of or the whole of the vulval area, extending to the groin.

Treatment of Thrush

Treatment of vulvovaginal candidiasis is usually easy without having to visit your doctor. Pharmacies stock clotrimazole creams and vaginal pessaries (medication that is put in the vagina) which will usually get rid of your symptoms.

You should see your doctor if you are not improving despite using these treatments. It is also advisable to see your doctor if you are having recurrent episodes of symptoms. It is now generally thought that this is not a case of getting constantly re-infected, but more likely that it is the original infection which is proving difficult to clear. In such a case, a more extensive approach may be needed to treat you. This can include prolonged prescription pessaries and creams, as well as tablets which, if taken on a monthly basis, can be useful (e.g. fluconazole 150 mg). Use of oral probiotics or vaginal boric acid pessaries have been suggested as being helpful for difficult cases of thrush, but these are as yet unproven. Some women respond well to a low sugar, low yeast diet. Screening for diseases such as diabetes may also be appropriate, as high sugar levels seen in diabetes encourages the growth of a fungal infection.

General measures to prevent thrush include:

- Wearing cotton underwear only, or cotton gussets to allow the area to remain well aerated

- Showering rather than soaking in baths for long periods of time
- Using *nothing* but water to clean the vulval area
- Using probiotics when taking antibiotics
- Avoiding wearing tight-fitting trousers or G-strings
- Avoiding using feminine hygiene sprays or powder in the area

If you have been having sex with condoms, treatment of your sexual partner is not thought to be helpful. Men will often get a transient penile rash and itch, but it is not thought to be responsible for re-infecting their female partner. However, clotrimazole cream for a few days is often enough to clear this, so it is probably worth considering if your partner has symptoms.

Bacterial Vaginosis (BV)

This is an extremely common vaginal infection. It is caused by several forms of bacteria, which normally live in the vagina without causing symptoms. Under certain conditions, these bacteria will overgrow, causing symptoms. The most common symptoms include a grey/white vaginal discharge with an unpleasant smell, and vaginal itch or soreness (especially after sex).

This is not a sexually transmitted infection (STI), although it is seen more commonly in women who have recently become sexually active (see below). If you are diagnosed with BV there is no need to treat your partner. Nevertheless, BV can behave like some serious STIs, such as chlamydia, gonorrhoea or trichomonas, so it is always worth getting it checked out by your doctor. BV will never cause pelvic pain or fevers, unlike some STIs.

Risk Factors for Developing BV

Like candidiasis, there are certain factors which will increase your chances of developing BV, and this may be related to the change in pH or acid/alkaline balance of the vagina. When the pH of the vagina becomes more alkaline, the vaginal bacteria are more likely to overgrow, causing symptoms. Causes of this include:

- Excessive washing of the vaginal area
- Antibiotic use
- New sexual partner or multiple sexual partners

Treatment of BV

BV is treated by way of antibiotics, either in oral form (metronidazole) or vaginal cream (clindamycin). The oral antibiotic is probably slightly better in treating BV, but should be balanced by the fact that it can cause some side effects, such as nausea. One course of antibiotics should be sufficient to completely treat the infection. However, recurrences can occur, and a second course of antibiotics can be used. In some cases, multiple recurrences happen, and this can be difficult to treat. In those cases, lifestyle changes need to be addressed, such as excessive washing of the vaginal area. In particular, it is important to avoid using any soaps or cleansing products, as these wash away the healthy bacteria. Additionally, condom use has been shown to reduce the incidence of BV. After an initial course of antibiotics, the use of oral probiotics and vaginal gels which acidify the vagina have also been shown to reduce the risk of recurrence.

Vulval Skin Problems

Lichen Sclerosus

Lichen sclerosus is a skin condition which primarily affects the genital skin, but can be found in non-genital areas. It is more common in women after they have reached the menopause, but it can occur in women of all ages. It is not well understood as to what the cause is, but it is thought to be an overactive immune reaction in the skin.

Signs and Symptoms of Lichen Sclerosus

Lichen sclerosus appears initially as small white spots on the vulva, which eventually start to increase in size. The skin affected is very thin and crinkly, often described as having a 'cigarette paper' appearance. Because the skin affected by this condition is also in poor condition, it is easily bruised, with a purplish appearance, and bleeds easily. If left untreated, scarring occurs, whereby the labia and vulva lose their typical folds and the vaginal opening can become very tight, making sex a problem. The main symptom, however, is a severe itch which persists and worsens. As the skin deteriorates, sores and bleeding can occur, as well as pain with sex.

Treatment of Lichen Sclerosus

Genital lichen sclerosus should always be treated, even if the symptoms are very mild. This is because the scarring seen with longstanding untreated lichen sclerosus is irreversible with local creams, and surgery may be needed once the condition has been adequately treated.

Treatment consists of strong steroid cream or ointment, which should be applied daily for approximately one month, after which the application of the steroid can be reduced. Maintenance treatment is usually several times per week. In postmenopausal women, local oestrogen may also be needed to improve the quality of the skin in the area.

Occasionally, a cream needs to be used which changes the immune reaction in the skin, if steroid treatment is not effective. Surgery to widen the vaginal opening may also be needed if extensive scarring has occurred.

In a small percentage of untreated lichen sclerosus cases, cancer will develop in the affected skin. The risk is reduced by treating the affected area with steroid cream, but six-monthly visits to your doctor are essential to check for this.

Lichen Planus

This is very similar to lichen sclerosus. However, it can affect skin anywhere in the body, including the mouth, and is less common in the vulval area. It is associated with an intense itch, and scarring if left untreated. It responds well to steroid cream application.

Vulval Pain

Vulvadynia

Vulvadynia is a condition of the vulva which is poorly understood. It can be defined as persistent pain in the vulval area without an identifiable cause, most commonly described as burning, stabbing or stinging. The pain can be unprovoked, or it can be initiated by sex, tight clothing, exercise or even sitting for long periods of time. The cause of vulvadynia is unknown, but it is often associated with a history of recurrent episodes of thrush, hormonal changes, and localised hypersensitivity or allergy. A history of sexual abuse is also associated with vulvadynia, but most women have no known contributing factors. It is also thought that an injury or irritation to the nerves supplying the skin of the vulva may be responsible for the condition, but this is still poorly understood.

Types of Vulvadynia

There are two recognised types of vulvadynia:

1. Vulvar vestibulitis syndrome – this is pain confined to the vestibule, or the area just at the entrance to the vagina.

Women with this variety will experience pain when pressure is applied to the vestibule, for example during sex, insertion of a tampon or during prolonged sitting.

2. Generalised vulvadynia – this is characterised by fairly constant pain, which can be anywhere in the genital area. It is typically worsened by pressure applied to the area.

Diagnosis of Vulvadynia

Vulvadynia is diagnosed by clinical examination. Your doctor will examine the area closely, looking for any signs of active infection, and swabs are recommended to check for fungal and bacterial infections. The vulva will usually appear normal in the case of vulvadynia. However, a cotton bud test can be used to demonstrate the hypersensitivity to pain that is felt in the affected areas. Your doctor will gently touch various areas on the vulva and vestibule with a cotton bud and ask you to indicate what level of pain is felt in various areas. This usually confirms the diagnosis.

Treatment of Vulvadynia

Treatment options for vulvadynia are based on relieving symptoms rather than a cure, as the cause or causes of vulvadynia are not well understood. These treatment options include:

- Antidepressants/anticonvulsants – in low doses some antidepressants, such as amitriptyline, can reduce the hypersensitivity in the vulval nerve endings.
- Local anaesthetic creams and gels
- Pelvic floor muscle therapy
- Nerve blocks
- Surgery – only in rare cases with vulvar vestibulitis syndrome

Bartholin's Abscess

The Bartholin's gland is located under the skin on either side of the vaginal opening. It is a gland which makes mucus needed for vaginal lubrication. A very small tube or duct leads from the gland to the vaginal opening through which mucus is secreted. However, in some women the duct becomes blocked with secretions and the gland becomes infected. A woman will experience increasing pain and swelling in the area over a few days, often very severe. There may be a fever as well. On examination, the side affected will appear swollen. If left untreated the abscess will usually burst itself, releasing pus and relieving a lot of the pain felt. However, it is unlikely that all the pus will have been discharged, and it may need further attention. Like any other abscess, it may need to be opened up a little under local anaesthetic and cleaned out. Sometimes antibiotics will help to settle the infection. In 10 per cent of cases, Bartholin's abscesses recur, and in those situations a surgical procedure called marsupialisation is necessary. Marsupialisation is where the abscess is opened, drained, and allowed to slowly heal from the inside out so that another abscess can never form again.

Psoriasis/Eczema

Like any other part of your skin, the vulva can be affected by common skin conditions, such as eczema and psoriasis. These conditions can cause a chronic itch, skin changes such as dryness and scaliness, and the skin can become secondarily infected if the area is being constantly scratched. The treatment of vulval psoriasis and eczema is similar to that for other skin, and the creams and general advice apply here too. The mainstay of treatment for both conditions is steroid creams applied directly to the affected skin.

Hidradenitis Suppuritiva

This is thankfully an uncommon condition but is seen in women from puberty onwards. It is a condition affecting the sweat glands of the groin and armpits primarily but can be seen elsewhere in the body. The sweat glands become blocked, and subsequent severe infection follows. It is not understood why this happens, but it is more common in obese women.

Hidradenitis suppuritiva typically appears as blackheads and painful red lumps under the skin. As these become infected they may discharge pus. Eventually, extensive scarring will occur. There is no cure for this unpleasant condition, but early diagnosis can prevent multiple infections, with the use of antibiotics, Dianette (a type of oral contraceptive), general cleaning techniques and, in some cases, retinoids to reduce oil production in the glands.

Key Points

- Thrush and bacterial vaginosis (BV) are the most common causes of vaginal discharge and discomfort.
- If recurrent thrush is a problem, long-term measures, such as probiotics and monthly antifungal medications, as well as some self-help measures, may be needed.
- Several skin conditions of the vulva can cause chronic itching and should be treated early; if left untreated, changes can be irreversible.
- Vulvadynia is a poorly understood, under-diagnosed cause of vulval pain, which can be improved with treatment.

18

Pregnancy

Pregnancy, to coin a phrase used by many, is a condition and not an illness. It is a huge topic, and countless books are dedicated to this subject alone. The antenatal care provided by your doctor differs from other interactions you may have had with them in the past. During pregnancy you more often than not feel and look well. However, the involvement of your doctor in your pregnancy from preconceptual care right through to your six-week postnatal check and beyond is crucial to making sure your pregnancy is safe and you are well informed at every stage. In this chapter I have covered the main areas of interest for women who are thinking about pregnancy, or who may be pregnant already. The topic of pregnancy would not be complete without covering miscarriage – sadly it is common in early pregnancy, affecting 20 to 25 per cent of all pregnancies.

Preconception Consultation

Making the decision to get pregnant is a very important one, and preparing yourself for conception is essential. It is always a good idea to see your doctor in advance of trying to get pregnant, as there may be health issues which need to be addressed to optimise your health.

Below are a few topics which need to be discussed with your doctor.

Existing Illnesses

If you have a pre-existing condition it is vital to meet with your doctor prior to conceiving to discuss the impact of your condition on your pregnancy and also on your own wellbeing. In the case of diabetes, your sugar control needs to be excellent at the time of conception to reduce any risk to the baby. In the case of hypothyroidism, your blood should be checked to ensure you are getting enough thyroid hormone, as inadequate thyroid hormone levels can cause a delay in conceiving. With antidepressant use, your doctor may want to change you to another type for conception and pregnancy.

Previous History of Pregnancy/Childbirth

A previous history of miscarriage, stillbirth, pre-eclampsia, premature delivery, diabetes in pregnancy and low birth weight are all conditions which may happen again in subsequent pregnancies, and your doctor should know about any past instances of these.

Folic Acid

It is recommended that you take 400 mcg folic acid supplements (available over the counter in pharmacies) daily for approximately four weeks prior to conception. This is to minimise the risk of neural tube defects (NTDs) such as spina bifida. If there is a history of NTDs in your family, your doctor may prescribe a 5 mg folic acid tablet.

Rubella Immunity

Your doctor may want to check your rubella antibody level. Rubella is a virus which causes devastating effects on an unborn foetus if you develop a rubella infection while pregnant. Most young women have been vaccinated against rubella and have sufficient antibodies in their blood to prevent an infection, which can be easily checked.

Smears

It is important to have had a normal smear in the two years prior to conception. If your smear is abnormal, your doctor may advise you to avoid getting pregnant until your smears have returned to normal. This only applies to significantly abnormal smears where the cells may need to be removed with a LLETZ procedure. Most mildly abnormal smears will resolve spontaneously and cervical smears can be resumed after delivery.

Alcohol and Recreational Drug Use

You and your partner's alcohol intake should be reduced if necessary around this time. Most importantly, the number of units of alcohol consumed at one sitting should be curtailed to less than 4 units at a time. Recreational drug use should be stopped.

Stopping Smoking

Smoking doubles your risk of having an underweight baby, and puts your baby's life at risk in some cases.

Risk of Inherited Diseases

If there are any inherited diseases within the family of either partner, such as cystic fibrosis, Huntington's disease or Duchenne's muscular dystrophy, the risks of your baby inheriting these should be discussed.

Advice on Obesity

If you are overweight or obese and considering getting pregnant, your doctor may advise you about trying to lose weight first. Being overweight or obese during pregnancy increases your risks of high blood pressure, diabetes and caesarean section, among other complications.

Advice on Fertile Times of the Month

Firstly, it may take a while, so don't panic if it doesn't happen in the first month. Up to 85 per cent of couples will conceive in the first year of trying. Having a good understanding of your cycle and when you are fertile will increase your chances of conceiving. You should know the average length of your menstrual cycle, i.e. the number of days from the first day of your period to the first day of your next period. Taking the total number of days, count backwards twelve to fourteen days, and that is your ovulation. For example, in a 28-day cycle, your ovulation is between day 14 and day 16; in a 26-day cycle, your ovulation is between day 12 and day 14; and in a 30-day cycle, your ovulation is between day 16 and day 18. It is best to have lots of sex before and around these days, rather than just on the exact day of ovulation. It is also a good idea to have sex two to three times per week outside the time of ovulation, in case you have a particularly long or short cycle that month.

Diagnosing Pregnancy

Most women, if they are actively trying to conceive, will be very aware if their period is late. Home pregnancy tests are now so accurate that they can often detect an early pregnancy before the period has even been missed. If you are doing an early pregnancy test, collect a sample of your urine first thing in the morning to maximise your chances of getting a positive result. The pregnancy hormone, HCG, which gives the positive result, is more concentrated in an early morning urine sample. If it is negative, try again two days later. The pregnancy hormone level doubles every 48 hours, so it should turn positive after this time if you are pregnant.

If you get a positive pregnancy test, you can calculate your baby's expected date of delivery (EDD) provided you have a reasonably regular cycle. It is calculated based on the first day of your last menstrual period (LMP), and 280 days are added to it. If you have an irregular cycle, your EDD is provisional, and should be confirmed with an ultrasound in the first fourteen weeks of pregnancy.

A woman's pregnancy is divided into three trimesters or time periods:

1. First trimester: conception to 12 weeks
2. Second trimester: 12–28 weeks
3. Third trimester: 28 weeks to delivery

First Visit to Your Doctor

Once you have had a positive pregnancy test it is a good idea to go and see your doctor. Some women want their doctor to repeat the pregnancy test for confirmation.

Your doctor will advise you on the following:

Various Options of Antenatal Care within Your Local Maternity Hospital

If this is your first pregnancy, it is likely that you have little or no knowledge of the various forms of antenatal care available to you. It is important to be informed of all your choices and any costs attached to each one.

Most hospitals offer several types, including:

- Public – this is antenatal care provided primarily by doctors in your local hospital, and is free of charge.
- Midwife-led – this is antenatal care provided by the midwives in your local hospital and is free of charge; in some cases, a home birth can be arranged with midwives in attendance.

- Semiprivate/private care in a public hospital – these are ante-natal care programmes which require private health insurance in place for at least 26 weeks prior to conception. Insurance companies only contribute a certain amount towards this level of care; the balance is paid by the patient.
- Semiprivate/private care in a private hospital
- Option of shared care between your hospital and your family doctor – this is a scheme where your antenatal care before delivery is shared between your doctor and a hospital obstetrician. This is also known as the Maternity and Infant Care Scheme. All women resident in Ireland are entitled to avail of this scheme. You are entitled to one visit before twelve weeks to diagnose your pregnancy, and six further visits ante-natally. It also includes two postnatal visits. This scheme is often much more convenient for the patient, as visits to their own doctor are quicker with less waiting time, and closer to their place of work or home. This service is free of charge to the patient. If you choose to opt for combined care with your doctor, an application form for the Maternity and Infant Scheme should be completed at this stage.

During a typical antenatal visit, your doctor should check the general wellbeing of the mother and infant, including assessing foetal movements, checking blood pressure, analysing a urine sample, examining your bump to assess the size of the baby and the way the baby is lying, and listening to the baby's heartbeat.

First Trimester Ultrasounds

Unfortunately, due to cutbacks in healthcare in recent years, ultrasound scans at your first visit to the hospital are not routine. It is advisable to try and have an ultrasound scan if possible before fourteen weeks, for several reasons. Firstly, it confirms the EDD, which is especially important if your menstrual cycle was irregular before conceiving. Secondly, it confirms an ongoing healthy pregnancy which gives couples the confidence to share their happy news with friends and relatives. Sadly, miscarriages do sometimes happen even after a normal scan, but this is very much the exception to the rule. Most of the maternity units provide a private ultrasound facility. Of course, if you are experiencing any pain or bleeding during the first trimester, an ultrasound is done in your local hospital free of charge.

Antenatal Screening for Chromosomal Abnormalities

This is testing which is done to detect chromosomal problems, such as Down syndrome, Edwards' syndrome and Patau's syndrome. It is not invasive and poses no risk to you or your baby. The test consists of an ultrasound scan of your baby's neck and a blood test from you, done between eleven and thirteen weeks. It is a screening test; in other words, it picks up a certain percentage of chromosomal problems, usually 90 per cent, but it will miss about 10 per cent. It is sometimes only offered to women over the age of 35 when the risk of chromosomal problems starts to increase. However, 80 per cent of Down syndrome babies are born to women under the age of 35, so it is important that women of all ages are aware of the screening test. If the screening test is highly suggestive of a problem, you will be offered chorionic villus sampling (CVS), which is an invasive procedure whereby a sample of the placenta is taken either through the abdominal wall or through the cervix and a diagnosis can be made. This runs the risk of causing miscarriage in one out of every one hundred cases.

General Lifestyle Advice

No alcohol should be consumed until the first trimester is over; in other words, twelve weeks from your LMP. After that, alcohol intake should be limited to 1 or 2 units per week. Most forms of exercise that you did on a regular basis before getting pregnant can be safely continued. Your diet should include fruit and vegetables; wholegrain breads and cereals; moderate amounts of low-fat dairy foods and lean meat; small amounts of food high in fat, sugar and salt; lean meat, chicken and fish; dried beans and lentils; nuts and seeds; low-fat milk, cheese and yoghurt; and leafy vegetables. A list of foods that should be avoided can be discussed at this stage, including unpasteurised products, soft cheeses, paté, uncooked shellfish, and any food containing raw egg. These foods have a higher risk of containing bacteria, such as campylobacter, listeria and salmonella. These can all cross the placenta and cause infection in the foetus, which can potentially lead to stillbirth and premature labour.

Miscarriage

Miscarriage is a heart-breaking aspect of what should be an incredibly happy event in a woman's life. No woman ever expects to miscarry, and the harsh reality of a miscarriage is an incredibly sad time for a couple. Unfortunately, it is very common, affecting one in five pregnancies in women under the age of 40, and as many as one in two pregnancies in women over the age of 40.

Most first trimester miscarriages occur because of a chromosomal abnormality. This occurs in a random fashion and, therefore, women are usually reassured that it is unlikely to happen again. Women who have had a first trimester miscarriage do not require any investigations. However, if you experience three consecutive miscarriages, it is possible that there may be another cause for the miscarriages, and certain investigations are appropriate at that stage.

Symptoms of a Miscarriage

The main symptoms of a miscarriage are cramp-like pain and vaginal bleeding. The bleeding varies from brown spotting to bleeding similar to a period. Likewise, the pain can range from extremely mild to severe. Women often report a loss of pregnancy symptoms.

Types of Miscarriage

- Threatened miscarriage – this describes mild bleeding and pain, but the pregnancy continues. More than 50 per cent of women with a threatened miscarriage go on to have a healthy, full-term pregnancy.
- Inevitable miscarriage – this means that a miscarriage will definitely happen. The doctor who examines you will feel the neck of the womb has opened and the pregnancy is over.
- Incomplete miscarriage – this is where some of the contents of the womb have come out, but some are still remaining inside. A small surgical procedure is often done to fully empty the womb.
- Complete miscarriage – the entire contents of the womb have been passed naturally by the patient. This is the most common outcome of a miscarriage.
- Missed miscarriage/blighted ovum – this occurs when the fertilised egg attaches itself to the lining of the womb but it fails to develop. The sac in which it lies continues to grow and pregnancy hormones are produced initially, leading to a positive pregnancy test and symptoms of pregnancy. In some cases you may experience spotting or cramps, or in other cases the blighted ovum is only discovered at a routine first trimester ultrasound.

What to Do if You Experience Bleeding

You should contact your doctor or your local maternity hospital if you are experiencing bleeding or pain in the first trimester. An ultrasound scan will usually be arranged. If you have been having a lot of heavy bleeding, the womb may be empty. In the case of a suspected blighted ovum, the pregnancy measurements will be much smaller than expected by your dates. However, in that case the ultrasound should be repeated seven days later to ensure that there has been no growth in the meantime and to confirm that this is indeed a blighted ovum. Sometimes you will miscarry in the meantime while waiting to repeat the scan. Depending on the results of the scan, your doctor will advise you as to whether any further medical treatment is needed at your local maternity hospital.

How Do You Treat a Miscarriage?

If you have had a complete miscarriage, no treatment is necessary. If you have had an incomplete miscarriage or a blighted ovum, there are several options. One is an evacuation of retained products of conception (ERPC), a day case procedure which is performed under full anaesthesia, where the womb is cleaned out. Another option is to take medication at home called misoprostol, which causes the neck of the womb to open and expel the contents of the womb. In some cases, an ERPC is more appropriate, when the vaginal bleeding is very heavy and the womb needs to empty quickly. For some women a surgical procedure allows them to get quicker closure on a distressing situation. Your options can be discussed with your hospital doctor. If you have taken misoprostol, the bleeding which follows will be heavy and more painful than your usual period. You may pass pale-coloured tissue as well as blood clots, which is foetal tissue.

What to Expect After a Miscarriage

Bleeding can persist for one to two weeks after a miscarriage, getting progressively lighter. Any pregnancy symptoms will disappear. Usually, you can expect your next period four to eight weeks after the miscarriage. If the bleeding is not settling, you should see your doctor. It is completely normal to feel emotionally drained and incredibly upset after you miscarry, regardless of how many weeks pregnant you were.

When Can I Try to Get Pregnant Again?

Every doctor has different advice about this. The truth is it depends on your individual circumstances. From a physical point of view, a lot of women will be fertile and ovulate two weeks after a miscarriage. There are no known risks to conceiving so quickly after a miscarriage. It certainly doesn't increase your risk of miscarrying again. Previously it was thought that conceiving before your cycle was restored to normal made dating the pregnancy difficult, but with modern ultrasound that is no longer a concern. The real question to ask yourself is, 'Are we emotionally ready as a couple?' Some are definitely not ready and need time to grieve for their loss and prepare themselves for conceiving again. Others feel the need to try again immediately.

Common Problems in Pregnancy

Pre-eclampsia

Pre-eclampsia occurs in 5 to 8 per cent of all pregnancies. It is a condition which develops swiftly and is characterised by high blood pressure and the presence of protein in the urine. Typically it presents after twenty weeks, and symptoms include generalised swelling, sudden weight gain, headaches and changes in vision.

However, some women with rapidly-advancing pre-eclampsia report few symptoms. Clinically, the signs are:

- Elevated blood pressure — more than 140/90 mmHg
- Proteinuria — more than or equal to +1 proteinuria when urine is tested with a dipstick

Water retention and swelling in the hands and feet is often seen in pregnancy and can be part of pre-eclampsia, but more often than not it is just a normal part of your pregnancy. If your doctor suspects you are developing pre-eclampsia, you will be referred to your local maternity unit. The treatment for pre-eclampsia is to deliver your baby: as soon as the baby is born the condition starts to resolve. If the pre-eclampsia is mild, you will be put under observation. If the preeclampsia is severe, then you may need to be delivered sooner rather than later. Sometimes you will need a few weeks of blood pressure tablets after the baby is born until everything returns to normal.

Gestational Diabetes

Gestational diabetes occurs in one out of every four hundred pregnancies. There are usually no symptoms, and it can be first detected on routine urinalysis, by the presence of persistently high sugar levels in the urine sample. The diagnosis is then made by a glucose tolerance test. This involves taking a sugary drink, and then having blood sugar levels checked for a few hours after. High risk groups, such as obese women, or women with a strong family history of diabetes, are screened at 28 weeks' gestation with a glucose challenge test. Management of gestational diabetes includes dietary advice and insulin if required.

Venous Thromboembolism (VTE)

VTE includes deep vein thrombosis (blood clot in leg or pelvis) and pulmonary embolism (blood clot in lung). Pregnancy increases the risk of VTE by five to tenfold. Other additional risk factors include the mother's age if over 35 years, obesity, caesarean section or immobility. Diagnosis of VTE in pregnancy can be difficult because of the normal changes which occur in pregnancy. Many of the classical symptoms, such as increased rate of breathing, increased heart rate, shortness of breath and leg swelling, can also be seen with a normal pregnancy. In up to a quarter of cases, an untreated leg or pelvic vein clot will progress to a pulmonary embolism. Identification of VTE is important, as it involves prolonged treatment for the original clot, preventive treatment during future pregnancies and avoidance of the oral contraceptive pill. The diagnostic test of choice is Doppler ultrasound of the leg veins and a special lung scan. However, in some cases where the test results are a little unclear, treatment is often started anyway.

Bleeding in Advanced Pregnancy – Placenta Praevia and Placental Abruption

Placenta praevia is a condition where the placenta attaches itself to the lower part of the womb, partially or totally covering the cervix. This is a common cause of painless bleeding later in pregnancy. It can cause a small or large bleed, but is characterised by the lack of pain or contractions associated with it. It is more commonly seen in women who have had previous caesarean sections or surgery to the womb.

When a woman has a bleed in pregnancy, regardless of the size of the bleed, an ultrasound is done to check the baby's wellbeing and the position of the placenta. If you have placenta praevia you may spend a significant amount of time in hospital until your delivery, in case you have further bleeding, which is very common. Because the placenta is covering the passageway to the outside world, your baby will need to be delivered by caesarean section in most cases.

A placenta which is lying low in the womb is usually detected at the routine second trimester scan. In most cases where the placenta is not completely covering the cervix, the placenta moves upwards during the rest of the pregnancy as the womb increases in size. A repeat scan in these cases is done in the third trimester, and the majority of these women can deliver normally.

Abruption of the placenta is an uncommon but potentially serious complication of pregnancy. It usually occurs in the third trimester, after 28 weeks. It occurs when the placenta comes away from the wall of the womb, causing vaginal bleeding and abdominal pain. It can be associated with sudden trauma to the abdomen, such as in seat belt injuries in a road traffic accident. It is also associated with cocaine use in pregnancy. The pain starts suddenly, and the amount of bleeding seen is not always a good indicator of how big the placental separation is. An ultrasound will detect most cases, but not all. Unless the abruption is very small, the safest treatment is to deliver the baby.

Anaemia

Anaemia is defined as haemoglobin (Hb) levels of less than 11 g/dl, and is more common in patients with multiple pregnancies and a poor diet. Symptoms include shortness of breath, pale colour, excessive tiredness and palpitations, but these are often confused with normal pregnancy symptoms. It is recommended that iron deficiency should be treated with low-dose iron supplements, such as ferrous sulphate 200 mg daily to maintain the haemoglobin level above 10 g/dl.

Nausea

Morning sickness can occur at any time of the day. It usually starts at six to seven weeks' gestation and lasts until twelve to fourteen weeks. In its more severe form – hyperemesis gravidarum – the patient may require hospitalisation for rehydration. Normally, a woman can cope with the unpleasant nausea by getting lots of rest, limiting herself to bland snacks and avoiding large meals.

Urinary Tract Infections (UTIs)

There is an 8 per cent increased risk of developing a UTI during pregnancy. This is thought to be due to increased progesterone levels, which cause the water passage or urethra to open up, and high levels of sugar in the urine of pregnant women, which encourages bacterial growth, increasing the risk of infection. Pregnant women can have infection without knowing it and, therefore, routine urine testing is important in pregnancy. Most pregnant women who develop a UTI will have cystitis, or infection of the bladder, which is simply treated with an antibiotic tablet. Much less commonly they may develop a kidney infection or pyelonephritis, which can make them very ill indeed. Those women often need to be admitted to hospital for intravenous antibiotics. All pregnant women should be treated when infection is detected in the urine, as severe kidney infections can cause problems in pregnancy, such as premature labour.

Constipation

Constipation is common during pregnancy for several reasons. Progesterone slows the passage of food through the gastrointestinal tract, while the growing uterus can put pressure on the rectum. Iron supplements can also make constipation worse. Drinking at least six to eight glasses of water a day, in conjunction with a diet rich in fruit and wholegrain foods, can prevent or relieve constipation.

Backache

This is due to several factors, including the increasing size of the womb and breasts, and also relaxin, the pregnancy-specific hormone that causes relaxation of muscles and tendons, particularly in the buttocks where the sacroiliac joints are found. Rest, local application of heat and, in some cases, physiotherapy can relieve backache. If severe enough, the patient may need pain relief.

Leg Cramps

The exact cause of these is unknown, but it may be related to changes in peripheral circulation, and also the extra weight being carried by the mother. The condition occurs most frequently in the second and third trimesters of pregnancy and can be relieved by stretching, walking, warm baths and massage.

Haemorrhoids or Piles

Haemorrhoids may first appear or worsen during pregnancy. They are caused by several factors, including constipation and back pressure on the veins in the abdomen caused by the pregnancy. They may also develop for the first time during the pushing stage of labour. The treatment of haemorrhoids is firstly prevention, by adhering to a high-fibre diet with lots of water. Symptoms can be improved with creams applied to the area, or suppositories inserted into the back passage. Most haemorrhoids resolve spontaneously following delivery but, occasionally, surgery is required.

Varicose Veins

Varicose veins are veins which are enlarged and distorted in shape. They are most commonly seen in legs and feet because of the pressure put on those particular veins due to standing and walking. The veins appear dark blue or purple, and are bulging through the skin. Most varicose veins do not cause symptoms and only affect the appearance of your legs. The smaller veins seen just under the skin are called spider veins. Symptoms of varicose veins include an ache in the legs, particularly after standing for long periods. Some women experience burning, throbbing or swelling.

Varicose veins can occur in anyone, but they are more likely to appear in women due to hormonal changes and pregnancy. They are more commonly seen as you get older, and they also tend to run in families. If you are standing for long periods of time or you are obese, you are more likely to develop varicose veins.

Most varicose veins cause little or no symptoms. Occasionally, in severe cases, skin ulcers can occur over the varicose vein, or a blood clot can occur in the varicose vein. The overlying skin gets red and hot, and this is known as thrombophlebitis. This is different to a deep vein thrombosis, which occurs in the deep veins of the leg, and is much more serious.

Weight loss, elevating your legs, wearing graduated compression stockings and avoiding standing or sitting for prolonged periods will all help to ease the discomfort associated with varicose veins. There are several procedures used to treat varicose veins, ranging from laser surgery, injecting the veins and vein stripping, where the whole vein is removed; these are all options depending on the size of the varicose veins.

Varicose veins that appear during pregnancy tend to resolve without treatment within a few months of delivery.

Postnatal Care

Support in the Immediate Postnatal Period

As part of the Maternity and Infant Care Scheme, you are encouraged to attend for a visit to your doctor two weeks after delivering your baby. After discharge from hospital, particularly on your first pregnancy, the prospect of caring for a newborn infant can seem daunting. Some of the common problems you may experience include exhaustion, tearfulness or low mood, backache, haemorrhoids and/or constipation, pain around your vulval and vaginal area. Feeding issues, such as mastitis, cracked or painful nipples and concerns regarding the baby's milk consumption and weight gain may also need to be discussed. This visit is an ideal time to ask your doctor about any concerns you might have about your own well-being or your baby's. Often, practical advice is all that is needed.

Six-week Check

Six weeks after delivering your baby, you are asked to attend your doctor again for a health check for you and your baby.

The following topics are usually covered:

- If you had high blood pressure or pre-eclampsia during your pregnancy, it is important to make sure that it has been resolved, as a small proportion of women affected in pregnancy will continue to have high blood pressure postnatally.
- If you are anaemic following delivery, you will probably be discharged from hospital on iron supplements. A repeat blood count may be appropriate if you are still pale, lightheaded or excessively tired.
- A breast examination may be needed if you think you may have mastitis.

- A pelvic examination is not always thought to be necessary, unless you are experiencing pain with sex or ongoing pain in the vaginal area.
- It is important for your doctor to ask about any incontinence to establish early on if there is a problem. Pelvic floor exercises are very important at this time, and if incontinence is an ongoing problem, a real effort should be made to make them part of your daily routine. Ongoing severe incontinence needs to be referred to a hospital gynaecologist.
- Any evidence of poor coping skills or mood depression at this point should be examined further to rule out postnatal depression.
- Contraception is an essential part of the visit. If you are still breastfeeding, your options are limited. Breastfeeding is not 100 per cent protective, even though you are not having periods. Barrier methods and the progesterone-only contraception are the most common forms used. The oral contraceptive pill cannot be used while breastfeeding, as the baby is exposed to the hormones through the breast milk. If your baby is being formula fed, a full range of contraception can be offered.

Key Points

- Preconceptual medical advice can be very helpful for couples thinking of embarking on a pregnancy.
- Miscarriage affects one in five early pregnancies.
- Most pregnancies are uncomplicated with only minor ailments.
- Bleeding in advanced pregnancy should always be investigated, no matter how small a bleed.

Useful Websites

Alcohol abuse – www.alcoholireland.ie

Anxiety and depression – http://www.mind.org.uk/help/ depression_and_anxiety

Cancer – www.irishcancer.ie; www.breastcancerireland.com; www. breastcheck.ie

Eating disorders – www.bodywhys.ie

Fertility – www.merrionfertility.ie; www.hari.ie

General women's health – www.women.webmd.com

Menopause – www.menopausematters.co.uk

Miscarriage – www.miscarriage.ie

Obesity and weight loss – www.irishheart.ie

Osteoporosis – www.irishosteoporosis.ie

PCOS – www.soulcysters.com

Premature menopause – www.daisynetwork.org.uk

Sexually transmitted infections – www.cdc.gov/std

Thyroid problems – www.nlm.nih.gov/medlineplus/ thyroiddiseases.html

Vulval and vaginal problems – www.anzvs.org; www.vulvadynia. com; www.vaginismus.com

Index

Index

high cholesterol
  management of 30
  and metabolic syndrome 31
  as risk factor of
    atherosclerosis 24
    heart attack 24, 29–30
    stroke 24, 29–30
    risk factors for 123
  as symptom of
    hypothyroidism 14
    polycystic ovarian syndrome
      (PCOS) 120
high grade squamous
  intraepithelial lesion (HSIL) 57
high temperature *see* fever
HIV *see* human immunodeficiency
  virus (HIV)
homeopathy 189
hormonal contraception 100–106
hormonal imbalance 214
hormone replacement therapy
  (HRT)
  description 189
  health benefits of 192–3
  methods of taking 190–91
  as risk factor of
    blood clots 195–6
    breast cancer 49, 163, 193–5
    breast cysts 35
    uterine cancer 61–2, 196
  side effects of 193
  stopping taking 191–2
  as treatment for
    osteoporosis 162–3, 189
    urogenital atrophy 153
  types of 189–90

hormone therapy 52–3
hot flushes 78, 153, 163, 183
HPV *see* human papillomavirus
  (HPV)
HRT *see* hormone replacement
  therapy (HRT)
HSG *see* hysterosalpingogram
  (HSG)
HSIL *see* high grade squamous
  intraepithelial lesion (HSIL)
HSV *see* herpes simplex virus
  (HSV)
human chorionic gonadotrophin
  (hCG) 79, 81
human immunodeficiency virus
  (HIV)
  description 90–91
  as risk factor of
    cervical cancer 55
    malignant melanoma 67
  testing for 91
  transmission of 90, 93–4
  treatment of 90
human papillomavirus (HPV)
  commonness of 86
  as risk factor of
    cervical cancer 53–4, 103
    genital warts 54, 87
  symptoms of 87
  vaccination against 58
hymen 230
hypercholesterolaemia *see* high
  cholesterol
hyperemesis gravidarum 261
hyperglycaemia *see* high blood
  sugar

Index

Index